A Country Cook's Kitchen

Traditional culinary skills, from breadmaking and preserving to curing and dairy

A Country Cook's Kitchen

ALISON WALKER

Additional recipes by Shona Crawford Poole

with photography by Tara Fisher

jacqui small

COUNTRY LIVING
MAGAZINE

First published in 2012 by
Jacqui Small LLP
An imprint of Aurum Press
7 Greenland Street
London NW1 0ND

ISBN: 978 1 906417 56 7

A catalogue record for this book is available from the
British Library.

2014 2013 2012
10 9 8 7 6 5 4 3 2 1

Printed in Singapore

Publisher: Jacqui Small
Managing Editor: Kerenza Swift
Art Director: Ashley Western
Project Editor: Abi Waters
Stylist: Caroline Reeves
Photographer: Tara Fisher
Production: Peter Colley

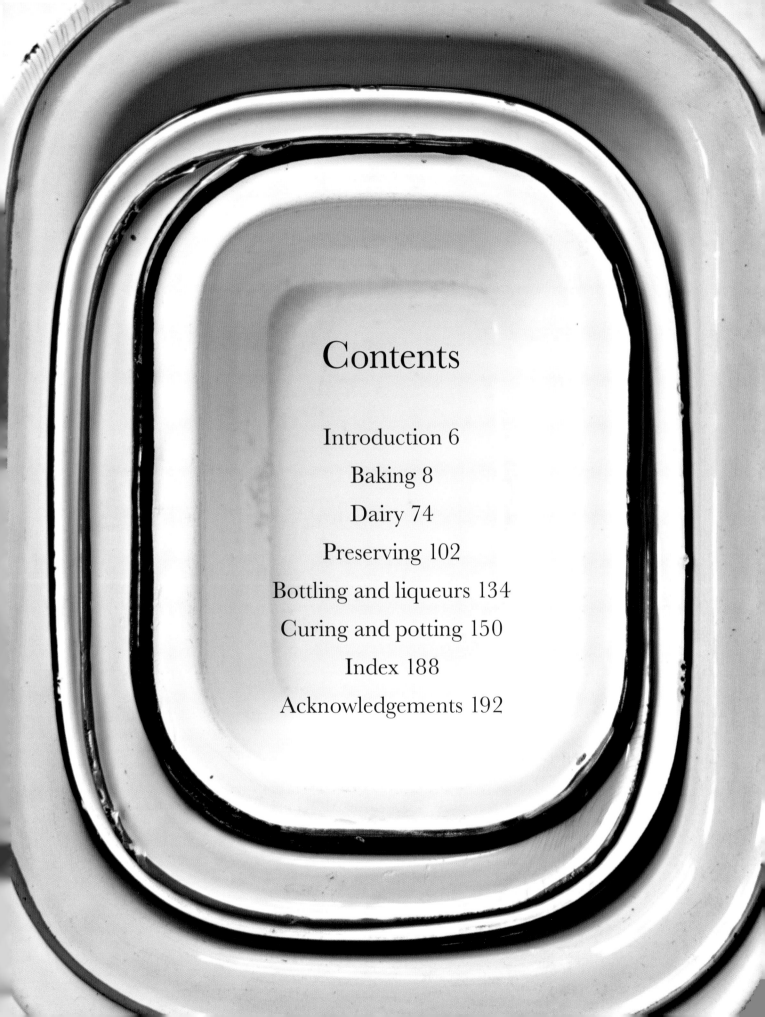

Contents

Introduction

Think of a traditional country kitchen and what comes to mind? A worn flagstone floor, an old-fashioned Windsor chair sitting snugly next to the warm, welcoming range cooker... My first thought is of a well-scrubbed, wooden farmhouse table laid out for tea, with feather-light scones, freshly churned butter, soft, creamy cheeses, glistening jars of jam made with berries from the garden – and all homemade, of course.

The kitchen skills needed to make this simple country fare is something our grandmothers and great-grandmothers would have taken for granted, family recipes passed down through generations of women who honed the dishes to perfection. As a child I loved to watch my grandmother making pies: she didn't own a pair of measuring scales or any fancy gadgets, everything was done by touch and experience. And, inevitably, those pies were perfect every time. Sadly, those kinds of skills have now been largely forgotten or fallen out of use, because, 'really, who has the time?' Who needs such things in a modern world where grabbing an expensive ready-meal for supper is the norm? That's understandable; of course we're too busy to churn butter or make our own cheese and why should we when we can pick up perfectly acceptable examples at the local shops? But where's the pleasure in that?

Every now and then, it's good to slow down and reconnect with Nature's bounty, enjoy the transformation of raw ingredients into an enticing plate of biscuits or mouth-watering sponge cake. I will happily spend many an hour turning a crop of just picked raspberries or a basket of hedgerow fruit into rows of jams and jellies to stock the pantry for the winter months, or turn out batches of fresh, meaty sausages for a Sunday cooked breakfast complete with a fruity chutney.

By using modern technology the old-fashioned techniques are easier to revive than you may think. I'm not asking you to laboriously make butter by hand in an antique butter churn – use a food mixer and it takes a fraction of the time – or keep your own pigs in the garden (find a good local butcher instead); just to simply enjoy some of the processes involved in making good food as well as the delicious end result. After all, what Victorian cook would have used a wooden spoon to make a sponge if she'd had access to electric hand-beaters! It's simple to incorporate country cooking into your life: you could bake a batch of bread for the week, then stock up the freezer with the surplus, while a country walk could turn into a forage for sloes to make a liqueur to give at Christmas.

Country cooking is close to my heart, the food I most like to prepare and share with family and friends. At its best, it's simple, hearty, thrifty, honest food that is a pleasure to create and a joy to eat. It enables you to cook amazing meals with cheaper ingredients, cope with garden gluts and, most importantly, know exactly the integrity of the food you are serving. With this in mind, I have covered everything I think the aspiring country cook needs to know, from the perhaps unfamiliar traditional skills of curing, bottling and cheese making, to the familiar old favourites like cake, bread and pastry making. Apart from a few recipes, very little specialist equipment is required. Step shots helpfully illustrate some of the trickier skills and each chapter covers in detail the equipment, ingredients and techniques you might need. My hope is that you will be tempted to delve in from time to time to make a chutney or cake, or to begin to adapt the skills of country cooking to fit your own lifestyle, even if it's only at weekends. Before long, you, too, can know the pleasure and benefits of eating your own bread, cheese or smoked fish...

Baking

Baking is surely at the heart of any country kitchen and gives the good cook a chance to shine, even with the simplest of recipes. Who can resist a batch of freshly baked scones warm from the oven? The comforting crunch of a homemade biscuit, a simple supper of fresh bread and cheese or a Victoria sponge filled with tangy raspberry jam is far superior to any shop-bought confection. They are a pleasure to make as well as eat, but the secret to success is to remember that baking is an exact science. Accurate weighing and the correct oven temperature are always vital.

Breadmaking

Breadmaking at home is a journey with new avenues and byways to explore at every turn. The more bread I bake, the more fascinating the process becomes. Yet what could be more basic than bread's four principal ingredients – flour and water, salt and yeast? With nothing more added than time and heat, the possible variations of crust and crumb, taste and texture, shape, size and style are quite literally innumerable.

From grain ground by hand, shaped into flat loaves and baked on hot stones, bakers down the ages have noted the effects of fire and the type and quality of grain on the end result. Through this, bakers have developed the breads we can choose today. Lucky us, except that for those of us with no decent local artisan bakery, the best we can buy is often factory-made bread. These loaves look good, stale quickly and will very likely be made with the usual additives that bedevil industrial production.

To bake your own bread is to know what it's made with; and that's just the beginning. Even if you never attempt more than one favourite recipe, every loaf will be subtly different. The heat of the kitchen affects how fast the dough rises – cooler and slower improves flavour. Only you can judge when the dough is ready for the oven. Bake it too soon and the bread won't rise to its full potential. Satisfaction of course is in the eating. How often do we salivate at the instruction: 'Serve with crusty bread'? Well here it is.

Left: Brown tin loaf

Opposite (from top to bottom):
Flowerpot rolls;
Cheese and cayenne bread sticks;
and Walnut and raisin bread.

INGREDIENTS

Flour is the main constituent of bread, usually strong wheat flour, which whether white or wholemeal, has plenty of gluten. This is the protein that when mixed with water unravels to form a cat's cradle of elastic strands that trap the gas created by yeast and raise the dough. The more you work with them, the more individual flours become. Even within a single tight category such as organic, strong wholemeal stoneground flour, the aroma and texture can be surprisingly varied. There are lots of functionally adequate flours available, but some flours are exceptionally fine – perhaps there is one milled locally to you? Check your local area to see if there are any local farms or mills producing organic flours – you will really notice the difference.

Rye, oats, barley, spelt, kamut and other grains can all be milled into flours. None has as much gluten as wheat, and many bake best in combination with it. Fresh is best for flour.

Yeast is the ingredient bakers get most irate about. There are great bakers who swear by fresh yeast and baking gurus who are just as happy with dried. Fresh yeast is pale and crumbles and should be stored in the fridge. Stale fresh yeast is darker, fudge-coloured and more plastic. So much of the fresh yeast sold in small wrapped blocks is stale before its use-by-date that a stock of dried (variously called 'quick', 'easy-blend' or 'fast-action') is prudent. It is wonderfully reliable and has a good shelf-life, but watch the use-by-date. Sourdough leaven is yeast in an ancient guise, but that's a whole other story.

Salt brings out the flavour of the bread and keeps the action of the yeast in check. Very little is needed so why not have the best, organic sea salt? If it has large flakes, grind it finely for breadmaking.

Water from the tap is fine in most locations.

Fat is used in small quantities in many recipes. A little butter or oil adds flavour, softens the crumb and improves the bread's keeping qualities.

EQUIPMENT

Bread's few ingredients need to be measured precisely and **accurate scales** are essential. When breadmaking by hand, I usually work with 1kg (2lb) flour at a time, enough to make two to three loaves, so I also need a **big bowl**. Earthenware is handsome and traditional. Stainless steel is cheap, and more usefully perhaps, lightweight.

One very simple tool mixes the dough, turns it out, divides it and cleans the worksurface as you knead and when you have finished – a **flexible scraper**. Mine is plastic and I can't work without it. Some breads are baked at the highest temperature your oven can rise to. Fitting it with a **baking stone**, a thick piece of granite or some other stone that will tolerate 230–250°C (450–482°F), allows the oven to hold its heat without dropping when the loaves are first put in. It took me a while to find an affordable stone, but eventually an architectural salvage yard produced a 3cm (1¼ inch) thick slab of black granite that is a good fit, and it lives permanently on the middle shelf of one of a pair of ovens. Professional bread ovens inject steam to allow the loaves to rise before forming a crust. Spraying a mist of water into the oven as you put the loaves in is the domestic alternative and needs only a **plastic spray bottle**. **Bread tins** and **oven sheets** should be heavy duty if they are not to scorch and warp respectively at high temperatures. A **flour shaker**, old or new, is useful. I keep a set of floured **cloths**, untainted by detergent smells, for shaping baguettes. Bowl-shaped **baskets** lined with linen are the real deal for proving round loaves, and earn their keep. And finally, if you are not getting the results you expect, check the heat of your oven with an **oven thermometer**.

A BIT OF TECHNIQUE (KNEADING)

Without a raising agent, in this case yeast, bread would be leaden and indigestible. The purpose of kneading dough is to activate the gluten in flour, helping the molecules of protein to stretch and wrap themselves around the gases produced by the yeast's fast breeding programme. There are various ways of doing this, including giving the job to a bread machine or sturdy food mixer fitted with a dough hook.

I have had success using the traditional British technique for kneading, strenuously pushing and folding the dough with liberal dustings of flour to stop it sticking. But I have made lighter and better bread since adopting a method of incorporating air into dough made with a higher proportion of water and no dustings of extra flour. If you are prepared to tolerate the sensation of glued-up fingers as the dough turns from a lumpen mess into a mass that is lithe and silky it is a skill worth cultivating (see page 14).

Yeast works efficiently at temperatures between 25–30°C (77–86°F). Too much heat kills it, and at 60°C (140°F) it dies. Refrigerating dough slows it down sharply, and freezing stops it in its tracks. When warmed up again, chilled or frozen dough carries on from where it left off.

Basic white dough

Once mastered, this basic recipe will enable you to create a variety of delicious breads and rolls with different toppings and glazes.

PREPARATION **15 MINUTES**
RESTING **AT LEAST 1 HOUR**

Makes enough for 2 medium loaves
**1kg (2lb) organic unbleached strong
   white flour, or French T55 flour
20g (¾oz) fresh yeast or
   10g (½oz) dried yeast or
   2 teaspoons fast-action dried yeast
20g (¾oz) sea salt
700ml (1 pint 3fl oz) warm water**

1 Put the flour in a bowl and crumble in the fresh yeast. Using your fingertips, lightly rub into the flour. (If using dried or fast-action yeast, mix it well with the flour.) Next add the salt and mix to distribute it.
2 Pour in three-quarters of the water and use a scraper to mix, adding the remaining water in one or two batches. As soon as the dough comes together and there is no loose flour in the bowl, turn the dough onto a clean surface to knead. Scrubbed wood is ideal, but any smooth hard surface is fine.
3 Gather together the dough using the scraper and, without flouring the worksurface, slide your fingers underneath it, leaving your thumbs on top. Pick up and pull the dough towards your body, lifting your hands to stretch it. Slap it down, throwing it away from you, then fold the dough remaining in your hands over the lower portion, trapping in air. Repeat the action of lifting, stretching and folding for about 5 minutes until the mixture is transformed from a sticky mass into a dough that feels alive in your hands. At first you will need to scrape it together from time to time, but as the gluten develops it starts to behave as a single, fairly co-operative entity.
4 Place the dough on a lightly floured surface. Shape it into a ball by bringing the edges to the middle, one at a time, and pressing them firmly into the centre. Turn the ball over and tuck it in.
5 To rest the dough and give it its first rise, lightly flour a bowl and put the dough into it, seam-side down. Dust the top lightly with flour to help prevent a skin forming, cover it with a clean cloth and place somewhere warm and draught-free for about 1 hour, or until the dough has doubled in volume. Now it is ready to shape, prove (the second rise) and bake.

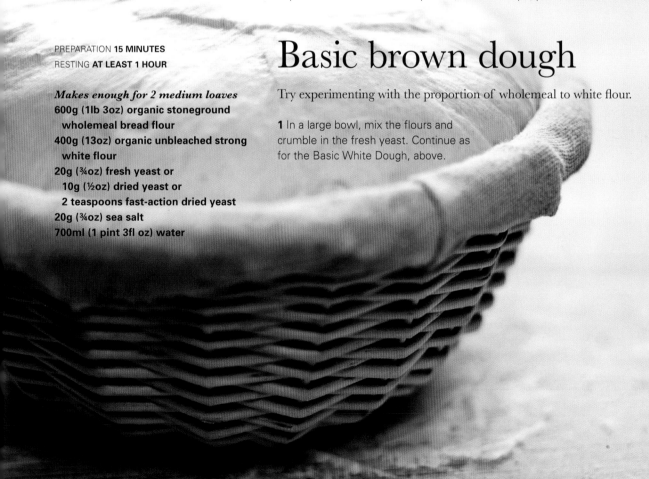

PREPARATION **15 MINUTES**
RESTING **AT LEAST 1 HOUR**

Makes enough for 2 medium loaves
**600g (1lb 3oz) organic stoneground
   wholemeal bread flour
400g (13oz) organic unbleached strong
   white flour
20g (¾oz) fresh yeast or
   10g (½oz) dried yeast or
   2 teaspoons fast-action dried yeast
20g (¾oz) sea salt
700ml (1 pint 3fl oz) water**

Basic brown dough

Try experimenting with the proportion of wholemeal to white flour.

1 In a large bowl, mix the flours and crumble in the fresh yeast. Continue as for the Basic White Dough, above.

Flowerpot rolls

These neat little rolls can be baked in real terracotta flowerpots that have been seasoned by brushing with oil and baking several times. Less romantically, and with less fuss, they can be baked in silicone pop-over moulds that look like extra-deep muffin cups.

SHAPING AND PROVING **ABOUT 1¼ HOURS**
COOKING **ABOUT 10 MINUTES**

Makes 12
oil, for brushing
**1 quantity rested Basic Brown Dough
  (see page 14)**
2 tablespoons pumpkin seeds, to finish

1 Heat the oven to 240°C (220°C fan oven/475°F), gas mark 9. Brush the inside of 12 small and seasoned flowerpots with oil and set them on a tray, or use silicone pop-over moulds, also set on a tray.
2 Turn the risen dough out of its bowl onto a lightly floured worksurface, using the scraper to help it on its way without too much stretching or tearing. Divide the dough into 12 equal pieces. Form each piece into a tight ball by repeatedly bringing an edge to the centre and pressing firmly, and drop them into the flowerpots or moulds. Cover and leave to prove until almost doubled in volume. Mist the tops with water and sprinkle with pumpkin seeds.
3 Mist the oven (see page 12) and slide in the tray. Reduce the heat to 220°C (200°C fan oven/425°F), gas mark 7 and bake for 10–12 minutes. Turn out of the moulds and cool a little on a wire rack. Serve warm.

Walnut and raisin bread

This recipe uses the basic brown dough with a little more yeast to counteract its enrichment with oil, nuts and raisins.

MIXING AND RESTING **ABOUT 1¼ HOURS**

SHAPING AND PROVING **ABOUT 1¼ HOURS**

COOKING **20 MINUTES**

Makes 2 small round loaves

300g (10oz) organic stoneground wholemeal bread flour
200g (7oz) organic unbleached strong white flour
15g (½oz) fresh yeast or 8g (¼oz) dried yeast or 1½ teaspoons fast-action dried yeast
10g (1 teaspoon) salt
350ml (12fl oz) water
2 tablespoons walnut oil
100g (3½oz) freshly shelled walnuts, coarsely chopped
100g (3½oz) raisins

1 Mix and knead the dough as for the Basic White Dough (see page 14). Add the oil, walnuts and raisins when the dough is almost ready to rest and continue kneading until they are evenly incorporated. Form the dough into a ball and rest in the bowl, covered, for 1 hour or until doubled in volume.
2 Preheat the oven to 220°C (200°C fan oven/425°F), gas mark 7. On a floured surface, divide the dough in half. Form each half into a ball and prove in floured linen-lined baskets (or bowls lined with floured cloths), covered, until almost doubled again.
3 Turn the loaves out onto a peel (a long-handled shovel) or tray (the base of a loose-bottomed cake or flan tin makes an impromptu peel for round loaves, and is easier still to use if lined with a circle of baking parchment). Mist the oven (see page 12) and slide in the loaves. After 5 minutes reduce the heat to 200°C (180°C fan oven/400°F), gas mark 6 and bake for 15 minutes more, or until they sound hollow when tapped.

Brown tin loaves

A traditional loaf shape, perfect for toasting. Like many brown breads, this one is even better the following day.

SHAPING AND PROVING **ABOUT 70 MINUTES**

COOKING **ABOUT 30 MINUTES**

Makes 2 medium tin loaves
1 quantity rested Basic Brown Dough (see page 14)
butter, to grease and wholemeal or rye flour, to dust

1 Preheat the oven to 240°C (220°C fan oven/475°F), gas mark 9. Prepare 2 non-stick loaf tins (20 x 13 x 8.5cm/8 x 5¼ x 3½ inches) by buttering them generously. If they are at all inclined to stick, flour them too.
2 Turn the risen dough out of its bowl onto a lightly floured worksurface, using the scraper to help it on its way without too much stretching or tearing. Divide the dough in half. Take one piece and flatten it into a rectangle. Fold one long side to the centre and press it firmly into place. Bring the other long side to the centre and press into place. Fold the long edge nearest to you onto the farther one and press firmly to seal the two together. Using your palms, roll the resulting sausage lightly to fit the tin approximately. Place the dough sausage, seam-side down, in a prepared tin. Shape the second loaf the same way. Cover the tins with a cloth and leave them in a warm, draught-free spot to prove until almost doubled in bulk – about 1 hour.
3 Dust the top of the loaves generously with wholemeal or rye flour and make a pattern of diagonal cuts on the tops.
4 Mist the oven (see page 12), place the tins directly on the baking stone or a baking tray and bake for 30 minutes. Turn the loaves out of their tins and tap them on the base. When they sound hollow they are done. If you are doubtful, return them to the oven for a few more minutes. Leave to cool completely on a wire rack before slicing.

Cottage loaf

This loaf is created using the traditional breadmaking method.

PREPARATION AND PROVING
ABOUT 2¾–3½ HOURS
COOKING **ABOUT 45 MINUTES**

Makes 1 loaf
15g (½oz) fresh yeast or 8g (¼oz) dried yeast or 1½ teaspoons fast-action dried yeast)
325ml (11fl oz) warm water
500g (1lb) strong white bread flour, plus extra for dusting
1½ teaspoons salt
oil, for greasing

1 Put the fresh or dried yeast in a small bowl with 100ml (3½fl oz) of the water and mash lightly with a fork. Leave for 5–10 minutes until frothy.
2 Put the flour in a large bowl and stir in the salt. (Stir in the fast-action yeast now, if using.) Make a well in the centre and pour in the frothy yeast mixture. Add the remaining water, mixing quickly as you go – you should have a soft, but not too sticky dough. Add a little more water if necessary.
3 Lightly flour a worksurface and knead the dough for at least 10 minutes until it is smooth and springs back when lightly pressed (see page 14). Put the dough in a large, lightly oiled bowl, cover with a cloth and leave to rise for 1½–2 hours until doubled in volume.
4 Briefly knead the dough for a couple of minutes to knock out any air pockets, then divide into two-thirds and a third. Briefly knead each piece and shape into a ball. Cover and leave to rest for about 10 minutes.
5 Preheat the oven to 200°C (180°C fan oven/400°F), gas mark 6. Put the large ball onto a lightly floured baking tray. Put the smaller ball on top and using two floured fingers push down through the centre joining the balls together. Cover and leave to prove in a warm place for 30–40 minutes. To test, lightly press the dough with a finger – if the dough springs back slowly it is ready to bake.
6 Generously dust the top of the loaf with flour and bake in the oven for 40–45 minutes until golden brown. Tap the bottom of the loaf and listen for a hollow sound – this means the bread is cooked. Cool on a wire rack.

Wholemeal soda bread

A quick-to-make Irish loaf that uses bicarbonate of soda rather than yeast as its raising agent.

PREPARATION 20 MINUTES
COOKING 30 MINUTES

Makes 1 loaf
175g (6oz) wholemeal flour
175g (6oz) plain white flour
½ teaspoon salt
25g (1oz) lard
1½ teaspoons bicarbonate of soda
3 teaspoons cream of tartar
1 teaspoon caster sugar
300ml (½ pint) buttermilk (see page 78)

1 Preheat the oven to 230°C (210°C fan oven/450°F), gas mark 8. Sift the flours into a large bowl, tipping in any bran left in the sieve. Stir in the salt, then rub in the lard. Stir in the bicarbonate of soda, cream of tartar and sugar.
2 Make a well in the centre and pour in the buttermilk. Quickly mix together with a wooden spoon and tip onto a lightly floured worksurface.
3 Shape very lightly into a ball and put on a lightly greased baking tray. Flatten slightly then, using the handle of a wooden spoon, mark a deep cross almost two-thirds of the way through. Bake for 30 minutes. Cool on a wire rack. Best eaten on day of baking.

Variations

• If you can't find buttermilk, stir 1 tablespoon lemon juice into 300ml (½ pint) whole milk.
• For a change, add 2 tablespoons mixed fresh chopped herbs, such as chives, parsley or rosemary, to the flour before adding the liquid.

Cheese and cayenne bread sticks

These are simple to shape and bake. With no need for butter, they are an easy bite-the-end-off bread for buffets, barbecues and picnics. Make up your own savoury, sweet or spicy variations to fit what's on the menu.

SHAPING AND PROVING **ABOUT 45 MINUTES**
COOKING **8–10 MINUTES**

Makes about 20
100g (3½oz) fine polenta
1 quantity rested Basic White Dough (see page 14) made with organic unbleached strong white flour
85g (3¼oz) freshly and finely grated Parmesan
1 teaspoon cayenne pepper

1 Preheat the oven to 240°C (220°C fan oven/475°F), gas mark 9. Dust one or more large oven trays lightly with polenta, and put the remaining polenta in a flat dish.
2 Turn the risen dough gently out of its bowl onto a lightly floured worksurface. Shape it into a large rectangle about 40 x 30cm (16 x 12 inches), lightly stretching the dough into a fairly even thickness. Scatter over the grated cheese, going right up to the edges, and dust evenly with cayenne pepper.
3 Fold one long edge over the middle third of the dough and bring down the other one over the top to make a three-layered dough sandwich.
4 Cut the roll into strips 2cm (¾ inch) wide, or a little less, using the scraper. Dip the cut edges of one strip lightly in the polenta, then twist it like barley sugar, at the same time pulling gently to lengthen it, and lay it on the prepared tray. Twist up the remaining pieces of dough the same way and lay them side-by-side on the tray, leaving enough space between them to allow for rising. Cover and leave to prove until almost doubled in volume.
5 Mist the oven (see page 12) immediately before and after putting the bread sticks into the oven. Bake for 8–10 minutes until golden and crisp. These are best eaten the day they are baked, but can be frozen and revived in a hot oven.

Baguettes

As an alternative to using French T55 flour, or strong white flour alone, try mixing equal quantities of strong and plain white flour when making baguettes.

SHAPING AND PROVING **ABOUT 1½ HOURS**
COOKING **20–25 MINUTES**

Makes 8
1 quantity rested Basic White Dough (see page 14)
flour, to shape

1 Lay a floured cloth on a baking tray, pleating it into ridges and furrows that will hold the shaped baguette, keeping them separate and supported as they prove. Preheat the oven to 240°C (220°C fan oven/475°F), gas mark 9.
2 Turn the risen dough gently out of its bowl onto a lightly floured worksurface. If you were now to roll pieces of this very soft dough into long sausage shapes, they would flatten and spread and not hold their shape in the oven. So here is how to put some backbone into the dough: the same technique is employed again when shaping the individual baguettes. Without knocking the air out of the dough, spread it into a rectangle. Lift the side nearest to you to the centre and press it down firmly. Bring the side furthest from you to the centre and press it firmly into place. Now bring the two long edges together and press them firmly together.
3 Divide the dough into 8 pieces weighing about 210g (7¼oz) each. Form each one into a ball and flour the top lightly. Rest it for 5 minutes.
4 Spread one ball of dough into a rectangle and repeat the shaping technique in step 2. The final seam will be the underside of the finished baguette. Using both hands and as little flour as possible on the worksurface, lightly roll the dough to lengthen it. Carefully lay the shaped dough, seam-side uppermost, into a furrow on the floured cloth. Shape the remainder of the dough balls, dust them lightly with flour and cover. Leave them in a warm place to rise until doubled in volume – about 1 hour.
5 I bake these loaves four at a time, and transferring the floppy lengths of dough safely into the oven is the trickiest part of the whole operation. A professional baker would use a peel (a long-handled shovel) and a technique honed with practice. You might find the following method easier. Line a large flat baking tray with baking parchment and flour it well. Roll four lengths of risen dough onto the prepared sheet, using the cloth rather than your hands to manoeuvre them, and space them out, seam-side down. Slash each baguette with 5 or 6 diagonal cuts, using a scalpel or razor blade, and a light assured touch.
6 Mist the oven (see page 12) to help form the loaves' crust. Now slide in the loaves on their paper onto the hot baking stone (see page 12), or if you haven't the nerve, tray and all. Give them another squirt of water, shut the oven door and bake for 10–12 minutes, until the loaves are golden and crisp. If the oven has a glass door you can watch the bread's development as it swells and rises, opening the cuts. This is bread you can eat straight from the oven as soon as it is cool enough to bite without burning your tongue.

A light rye loaf

Increase the proportion of rye to white flour if you prefer a denser loaf.

PREPARATION **25 MINUTES PLUS RISING**
COOKING **45 MINUTES**

Makes 2 loaves

15g (½oz) fresh yeast or
 8g (¼oz) dried yeast or 1½ teaspoons
 fast-action dried yeast
½ teaspoon caster sugar
200g (7oz) strong white bread flour
300g (10oz) rye flour, plus extra for
 dusting
1½ teaspoons fine sea salt

1 Combine the fresh or dried yeast in a bowl with 150ml (¼ pint) hand-hot water and the sugar. Leave to stand for 10 minutes. Stir in half of the white flour until combined. Cover and leave for 2 hours until bubbly.

2 Measure out another 250ml (8fl oz) hand-hot water. In another large bowl, mix together the remaining white flour with the rye flour and salt. (Add the fast-action yeast now if using.) Make a well in the centre and pour in the yeast mixture and two-thirds of the water. Mix together to form a soft and fairly sticky dough. Add more water if necessary.

3 Turn out onto a lightly floured worksurface and knead for 10 minutes until smooth and elastic.

4 Put the dough into a lightly oiled bowl and cover with a cloth. Leave to rise until doubled in volume – about 1–1½ hours. Knock back and leave to rest for 5 minutes covered with the upturned bowl.

5 Divide the dough in half and shape into 2 loaves about 30cm (12 inches) long, tapering them slightly at each end. Transfer to a large, lightly floured baking tray. Lightly dust with rye flour. Using a very sharp knife, make diagonal slashes down the length of the loaves at regular intervals. Cover and leave to prove for 1–1½ hours until doubled in volume.

6 Preheat the oven to 200°C (180°C fan oven/400°F), gas mark 6. Bake the loaves for 45 minutes until golden. They should sound hollow when tapped on the base. Cool completely on a wire rack before slicing.

Crumpets

Crumpets freeze well and should be toasted after defrosting.

PREPARATION **30 MINUTES PLUS RISING**
COOKING **35 MINUTES**

Makes 12

200ml (7fl oz) milk
15g (½oz) fresh yeast or
 8g (¼oz) dried yeast or 1½ teaspoons
 fast-action dried yeast
1 teaspoon caster sugar
250g (8oz) strong white bread flour
250g (8oz) plain white flour
2 teaspoons salt
2 tablespoons sunflower oil
1 teaspoon bicarbonate of soda
550ml (17½fl oz) warm water

1 Scald the milk until hot, then leave to cool until tepid.

2 Mix together the fresh or dried yeast with the milk and the sugar. Leave for 5–10 minutes until frothy.

3 Sift the flours into a large bowl. Stir in the salt. (Add the fast-action yeast now, if using).

4 Make a well in the centre and pour in the frothy yeast mixture, oil and 400ml (14fl oz) of the warm water. Beat until it makes a smooth and elastic batter.

5 Cover with a cloth and leave for 1½–2 hours until the mixture rises and the surface is covered with bubbles.

6 Dissolve the bicarbonate of soda in the remaining warm water and stir it into the batter. Cover and leave for 30 minutes.

7 Put a large frying pan over a medium to low heat. Lightly grease three or four 8cm (3½ inch) metal ring moulds and put into the pan. Pour the batter into the rings until three-quarters full and cook for about 8 minutes until the top sets and bubbles have formed on the surface.

8 Turn over in the moulds, pushing the crumpet down onto the pan base and cook for 4 minutes until golden. Keep warm in a low oven. Repeat until the batter is used up.

9 Serve warm with butter and preserves. The crumpets can also be toasted.

Pastry

Homely savoury and sweet pies, delicate pastries and warming winter puddings, where would we be without the crumbly, flaky, utterly delicious pastry encasing them? Before cooks perfected the art of pastry making, it was simply a vehicle for the filling, something to be tossed away once the middle was eaten. Happily for the country cook, someone long ago discovered how to make featherlight pastry that deserved to be eaten for its own sake. Indeed, some would argue that it's the best bit and when made well it is a culinary triumph. Don't let that scare the novices among you: follow the steps carefully and you'll discover how achievable and delicious homemade pastry really is.

A soggy base?
Fruit pies often suffer from soggy pastry bottoms due to their moist fillings. To prevent this: brush the base before filling with lightly whisked egg white to make a seal; or sprinkle 1 tablespoon fine semolina on the bottom to absorb juices; or toss the fruit in 1 tablespoon plain flour beforehand.

INGREDIENTS

Low in gluten, **soft wheat flour** is best for pastry making. **Wholemeal flour** makes a nutty-tasting but heavier dough; use it half and half with white to give lighter results. Good-quality **butter** adds flavour while **lard** produces a flaky crust that's especially tasty for meat pies. Vegetarians and vegans can replace animal fats with **vegetable shortening**. Adding **egg** to a shortcrust mix gives a crumbly rich texture. Beat the egg yolk into the amount of water specified in the recipe before adding to flour: this stops eggy streaks ruining the appearance of the dough. **Water** should always be ice cold: it ensures pastry is crumbly (short) and produces steam for rise in flaky pastry. Go easy though because adding too much will make it tough. Stir in a little **caster** or **icing sugar** to add sweetness and colour, or a hint of **vanilla extract**, **citrus zest** and ground **spices**, such as cinnamon, nutmeg and ginger. **Herbs**, ground **almonds**, **hazelnuts** and **walnuts** and **sesame** and **poppy seeds** add texture and taste. A pinch of **salt** is essential to heighten flavour.

EQUIPMENT

Cool hands and **light fingers** are all you need to make good pastry but a few other pieces of equipment will make life easier. A **rolling pin** is the most useful: choose from traditional wood or marble, silicone or glass. There are even antique versions that can be filled with cold water to ensure pastry is kept cool while rolling. If you plan to make pastry regularly, invest in a **marble slab** for rolling out – they're inexpensive and stay cool in hot weather. For crisper results, **metal flan tins** conduct heat more efficiently than ceramic dishes. Cookshops sell ceramic **baking beans** for baking blind but a mixture of rice and dried beans work just as well. Chill **bowls** and other equipment before you begin, especially in hot weather. Pastry doughs can also be prepared in a **food processor** but be careful not to overprocess.

A BIT OF TECHNIQUE

• Work quickly and lightly and always chill dough after working to relax the gluten and set the fat. It will make the dough easier to roll later.
• When rolling out, use the minimal amount of flour on the worksurface and use short, sharp strokes. Give the pastry a quarter turn every few strokes.
• Chill the pastry case thoroughly or freeze until very firm before baking. Don't skip this step: the fat in the dough needs to be very cold so that it doesn't melt in the oven before the pastry has had a chance to set. If you've watched your pastry slide down the edges of the tin before, this was probably because you didn't let it get cold enough prior to baking.

LINING TIPS

If lining a pie dish or tart tin, don't try to pick up the rolled out pastry in one large piece – it is more likely to split or crack. Instead, roll it loosely around the rolling pin and slide the dish or tin underneath (see pictures, page 28). Carefully unroll the pastry across the dish, then ease the dough into the tin, pressing it into the corners or edges. At this stage, I like to leave pastry to sit in the tin for a few minutes before trimming the edges – it allows the gluten to relax, making the pastry less likely to shrink at the edges during cooking.

BAKING BLIND

When making tarts, shortcrust pastry is often baked blind (partially cooked) before the filling is added, otherwise the moisture from the filling would prevent the pastry crisping sufficiently, resulting in a soggy base. So the pastry case can be partially cooked before a filling is added, then cooked further as in the case of a savoury tart; or the case is fully cooked until crisp, cooled and then filled with a sweet filling that needs no further cooking, such as custard or cream and fruit.

To bake blind, line the tart tin with the pastry as specified above or in the recipe. Prick the base all over with a fork and line with a crumpled circle of baking parchment that is slightly larger in diameter than the pastry case. Fill with enough baking beans to support the sides of the pastry with a layer in the centre to stop it puffing up. Bake for about 12–15 minutes in an oven preheated to 200°C (180°C fan oven/400°F), gas mark 6, until the sides are set. Remove the baking beans and baking parchment, then return to the oven for 5–10 minutes until the base is sandy to the touch.

Basic shortcrust pastry

As a general rule, shortcrust is made with half the amount of fat to flour.

PREPARATION **15 MINUTES PLUS CHILLING**

Makes about 250g (8oz) dough
175g (6oz) plain white flour
a pinch of salt
55g (2¼oz) cold butter, diced
30g (1¼oz) cold lard, diced
3 tablespoons ice-cold water

1 Sift the flour into a bowl with the salt. Rub in the fat between your fingertips until the mixture resembles fine breadcrumbs. If the mixture starts to look oily, pop the bowl in the fridge and resume when the fat has re-chilled. Sprinkle over most of the water and bring together the mixture into lumps with a flat-bladed table knife. Sprinkle a few drops of the remaining water over any dry areas and bring those together too. Don't add the water all at once as too much results in tough pastry.
2 Bring together the lumps with your fingertips and gently knead together to form a smooth disc.
3 Wrap closely in cling film and chill for 30 minutes before rolling and shaping.
4 Flour the worksurface and roll out the pastry, giving quarter turns.
5 Roll the pastry around the rolling pin, slide the tart or pie tin underneath and gently unroll the pastry. Ease it into the sides. Trim the edges with a sharp knife and prick the base with a fork. Chill.
6 Line the tart and blind bake following the instructions on page 26 or according to the recipe you are following.

Variations

• To make rich shortcrust, use all butter and mix 1 egg yolk with 2 tablespoons ice-cold water.
• To make sweet shortcrust, stir in 2 tablespoons caster sugar after the butter has been rubbed in.

Egg and bacon tart

This classic tart is made with just a few simple ingredients. For a change, replace the bacon with smoked ham and the Gruyère with a strong Cheddar.

PREPARATION **40 MINUTES PLUS CHILLING**
COOKING **ABOUT 1 HOUR**

Serves 6
1 quantity Basic Shortcrust Pastry
(see page 28)
125g (4oz) smoked streaky bacon,
derinded and diced
75g (3oz) Gruyère, grated
2 medium eggs, beaten
150ml (¼ pint) single cream
salt and freshly ground black pepper

1 Roll out the pastry and use it to line a 20cm (8 inch) flan tin. Chill for 30 minutes, preheat the oven to 200°C (180°C fan oven/400°F), gas mark 6 and then bake blind (see page 26).

2 Turn down the oven temperature to 180°C (160°C fan oven/350°F), gas mark 4 and put a baking sheet in the oven to preheat. Sprinkle the bacon over the base of the pastry case, followed by the cheese.

3 Beat together the eggs and cream with plenty of seasoning and pour into the pastry case. Bake in the oven on the preheated baking sheet for 30–40 minutes until the filling is risen and golden. Serve hot or cold.

Maple pecan pie

If you can't find molasses sugar, use dark brown muscovado sugar instead.

PREPARATION **35 MINUTES PLUS CHILLING**
COOKING **ABOUT 1 HOUR**

Serves 6–8

1 quantity Basic Rich Shortcrust
   pastry (see page 28) made with
   225g (7½oz) flour and 110g (3½oz)
   cold butter
75g (3oz) butter
75g (3oz) molasses sugar
3 medium eggs, beaten
1 teaspoon cornflour
200g (7oz) pecan halves
60ml (2½fl oz) dark maple syrup
250ml (8fl oz) golden syrup
1 teaspoon vanilla extract

1 Roll out the pastry and use it to line a 23cm (9 inch) flan tin. Chill for 30 minutes, preheat the oven to 200°C (180°C fan oven/400°F), gas mark 6 and then bake blind (see page 26).
2 Turn down the oven temperature to 180°C (160°C fan oven/350°F), gas mark 4 and put a baking sheet in the oven to preheat. Beat the butter and sugar together until soft and fluffy, then gradually beat in the eggs with the cornflour.
3 Stir in two-thirds of the pecans, the syrups and vanilla extract and pour into the pastry case. Arrange the remaining pecan halves on top.
4 Bake in the oven on the preheated baking sheet for 45 minutes until the filling is set. Serve warm.

Basic suet pastry

Suet pastry is used to make savoury and sweet steamed puddings. Commercial suet is dusted in rice flour to keep the granules separate. If using fresh butcher's suet, add a sprinkle of flour after grating.

PREPARATION **15 MINUTES**

Makes about 500g (1lb) dough
300g (10oz) self-raising flour
a large pinch of salt
175g (6oz) beef or vegetable suet
butter, for greasing

1 Sift the flour into a large bowl with the salt. Stir in the suet. Sprinkle with 2–3 tablespoons ice-cold water and bring together with a flat-bladed knife to make a soft, but not sticky dough.
2 If lining a pudding basin, roll out the pastry into a large circle about 5mm (¼ inch) thick. Cut away about one-third of the pastry (as shown above); set aside. Grease the basin and line with the larger piece of pastry by bringing together the two cut edges so that they overlap slightly (into a basin shape); press firmly to seal. Add your chosen filling.
3 Roll out the remaining pastry into a circle and brush the edges with water. Seal on top of the pastry lining and trim. Cover with a lining of greaseproof paper and foil, pleated down the centre. Secure with string and trim away the excess paper and foil so that it won't sit in the pan water.

4 Put the basin on top of an upturned saucer placed in a large pan. Pour in enough boiling water to come halfway up the sides of the basin, cover and bubble gently until cooked. Do not let the water boil dry. Alternatively, cook in a steamer. (See individual recipes for cooking times.)

Steak and mushroom pudding

PREPARATION **30 MINUTES**
COOKING **6–7 HOURS**

Serves 4

600g (1lb 3oz) braising beef, trimmed and cut into bite-sized pieces
275g (9oz) small button mushrooms
½ tablespoon seasoned flour
1 quantity Basic Suet Pastry (see page 31)
1 small onion, finely chopped
½ tablespoon finely chopped parsley
salt and freshly ground black pepper

Once this pudding is on the hob, it will sit happily cooking all day, but check regularly to see if the water level needs topping up.

1 Lightly toss the beef and mushrooms in the flour. Shake off the excess.
2 Line a 1 litre (1¾ pint) pudding basin with two-thirds of the pastry (see page 31). Fill the basin with the meat and mushrooms, layering with the onion, parsley and plenty of seasoning as you go.
3 Pour in enough water to fill the pastry case by two-thirds. Seal with a suet pastry lid (see page 31). Steam immediately for 6–7 hours (see page 31). Turn out onto a serving plate and serve with seasonal vegetables if liked.

Marmalade steamed pudding

To vary the recipe, swap the marmalade for jam or mincemeat.

PREPARATION **30 MINUTES**
COOKING **2 HOURS**

Serves 6
zest of 1 orange
1 quantity Basic Suet Pastry (see page 31)
1 x 454g (14½oz) jar thick-cut marmalade (or for homemade recipes see pages 104–111)
1 tablespoon whisky (optional)
custard or cream, to serve

1 Stir in the orange zest to the pastry mix before adding the water. On a lightly floured worksurface, roll out to a 30cm (12 inch) square.
2 Spread over the marmalade and sprinkle with the whisky, if using.
3 Roll up the pastry tightly from one long end. Cut into 2cm (¾ inch) slices. Line the bottom and sides of a greased 1 litre (1¾ pint) pudding basin with slices of the pastry, cut sides outwards. Fill the centre with remaining slices. Cover with a layer of pleated greaseproof paper and foil and tie with string. Steam immediately for 2 hours (see page 31). Turn out onto a plate and serve with custard or cream.

Left:
Top left: shape the pastry over upturned jam jars;
Bottom: wrap greaseproof paper around the pies to keep their shape while cooking;
Top right: once topped with lids, cut a small hole to let out steam.
Below: the cooked pies are filled with stock.

Basic hot-water crust pastry

Use jam jars, a soufflé dish or any round straight-sided dish as a mould for the pastry.

PREPARATION **40 MINUTES**

Makes about 250g (8oz) dough
225g (7½oz) plain white flour
½ teaspoon salt
50g (2oz) lard
100ml (3½fl oz) water
beaten egg, to glaze

1 Warm a mixing bowl and your chosen mould before using. Sift the flour into a bowl with ½ teaspoon salt. Make a well in the centre. Put the lard into a pan with 100ml (3½fl oz) water and bring to the boil. Pour into the well in the flour, then gradually work the flour into the centre with a wooden spoon. Beat until combined, then knead until smooth on a lightly floured worksurface.

2 Cut off one-third of the pastry to make a lid(s) and keep warm by setting on a plate over a bowl of hot water and covering with a cloth.

3 Roll out the remaining pastry into a circle 2cm (¾ inch) larger than the base of your mould and sit the mould in the centre. Turn over the mould so that the pastry is sitting on the top and then use your hands to mould the pastry down to a thickness of about 6mm (¼ inch) – the pastry should still be warm to make moulding easier.

4 Turn over the mould, wrap a double strip of greaseproof paper around the sides and tie with string. Remove the mould. Add the meat filling. Dampen the inside edge, then roll out the remaining pastry to form a lid(s) that sits up to the inner edges. Crimp to seal. Make a hole in the lid to let steam escape. Decorate with pastry trimmings if you like. Glaze with beaten egg, chill, then glaze again before baking.

Individual game pies

Homemade stock should contain enough gelatine to set in the pie. If using bought stock, use 1 teaspoon powdered gelatine following the packet instructions.

1 Put the game in a non-metallic bowl with the Madeira or port, mace and thyme. Marinate overnight in the fridge.

2 Mix together the marinated game, sausagemeat, onion and garlic. Season well and chill. Preheat the oven to 200°C (180°C fan oven/400°F), gas mark 6.

3 Divide two-thirds of the pastry into 6 pieces. While working on one piece, keep the others warm. Roll out and mould around a cling-filmed-covered 450g (14½oz) jam jar so they are about 7cm (3 inches) high. Repeat with the 5 other pieces. Wrap with greaseproof paper and secure. Remove the jars and cling film and fill the pastry cases with the meat, packing in firmly as it will shrink during cooking (see page 34).

4 Divide the remaining pastry into 6 pieces and roll out lids (see page 34).

Seal the pies and crimp. Cut steam holes and glaze the tops with beaten egg. Chill for 30 minutes.

5 Glaze again with beaten egg. Bake for 20 minutes, then turn down the oven temperature to 180°C (160°C fan oven/350°F), gas mark 4. Remove the greaseproof paper, brush the sides with beaten egg and cook for another 40 minutes. To check the meat is cooked through, put a skewer into the centre of the meat through the steam hole. Hold it there for 10 seconds, then test the temperature on the back of your wrist. If it is hot the meat is cooked; if not return to the oven for 10 minutes and check again. Cool on a wire rack. When the pies are at room temperature, pour in the stock through the steam holes. Leave to set in the fridge.

PREPARATION **40 MINUTES**
COOKING **1 HOUR PLUS OVERNIGHT MARINATING, CHILLING AND SETTING**

Makes 6 pies

750g (1½lb) mixed game, cubed, such as rabbit, venison and pheasant
4 tablespoons Madeira or port
½ teaspoon ground mace
2 teaspoons thyme leaves
225g (7½oz) pork sausagemeat
½ onion, finely chopped
2 garlic cloves, crushed
2 quantities Basic Hot-water Crust Pastry (see page 34)
1 egg, beaten
1.1 litres (1¾ pints) game stock
salt and freshly ground black pepper

Basic flaky pastry

Make a few batches of this pastry in one session and freeze any that you don't use straight away. Defrost in the fridge overnight before rolling and shaping.

PREPARATION **50 MINUTES PLUS CHILLING**

Makes about 400g (13oz) dough
225g (7½oz) plain white flour
a large pinch of salt
75g (3oz) butter, diced and at room
    temperature
6 tablespoons ice-cold water
75g (3oz) lard, diced and at room
    temperature

1 Sift the flour and salt into a large bowl. Rub in half of the butter until the mixture resembles breadcrumbs. Sprinkle over the water and quickly bring together into clumps with a flat-bladed knife. Bring together with your fingertips and work into a soft, but not sticky dough.
2 Shape into a rectangle and wrap in a layer of greaseproof paper and cling film. Chill for 10 minutes to relax.
3 On a lightly floured worksurface, roll the dough into a 15 x 30cm (6 x 12 inch) rectangle. Dot half of the lard over the top two-thirds of the pastry.
4 Fold the bottom third up to the middle and the top third down to make a parcel.

Brush away excess flour on the dough as you do so. Gently mark the edges with a rolling pin to seal.
5 Turn so the long sealed edge is on your left-hand side, roll and fold as before but without any fat. Chill for 20 minutes.
6 Roll again and dot with the remaining butter as before. Chill.
7 Roll again and dot with the remaining lard as before. Chill.
8 Roll again without fat and chill.
9 Preheat the oven to 200°C (180°C fan oven/400°F), gas mark 6. Now the dough is ready to roll, shape as required and bake (see recipes opposite).

Sausage and apple plait

Use a tart apple to cut through the fattiness of the meat.

PREPARATION **20 MINUTES PLUS CHILLING**
COOKING **55 MINUTES**

Serves 8
20g (¾oz) butter
1 small onion, finely chopped
1 small dessert apple, peeled, cored and diced
450g (14½oz) pork sausagemeat
150g (5oz) fresh breadcrumbs
8 sage leaves, chopped
1 tablespoon wholegrain mustard
1 quantity Basic Flaky Pastry (see page 36)
beaten egg, to glaze

1 Melt the butter in a pan and gently cook the onion for
10 minutes until softened. Cool. Mix together the cooled onion
with the apple, sausagemeat, breadcrumbs, sage and mustard.
2 Roll out the pastry to a rectangle 3mm (⅛ inch) thick. Place
the sausagemeat down the centre. Make horizontal cuts in the
pastry 2cm (¾ inch) apart at right-angles to the meat.
3 Brush the edges with egg and fold the pastry into the centre
overlapping as you go. Brush with more beaten egg and chill
for 30 minutes.
4 Preheat the oven to 220°C (200°C fan oven/425°F), gas
mark 7. Place the plait on a heavy baking sheet and brush
with more beaten egg. Bake for 15 minutes, then reduce
the oven temperature to 200°C (180°C fan oven/400°F), gas
mark 6 and bake for another 30 minutes until golden. Serve
warm, cut into slices.

Spiced fruit pastries

Eat these warm from the oven and you'll understand why
it's worth going to the effort of making flaky pastry.

PREPARATION **25 MINUTES**
COOKING **15 MINUTES**

Makes 8 pastries
25g (1oz) butter
125g (4oz) currants
1 tablespoon mixed peel
50g (2oz) soft light brown sugar
½ teaspoon mixed ground spice
1 quantity Basic Flaky Pastry (see page 36)
egg white, to glaze
caster sugar, for sprinkling

1 Preheat the oven to 220°C (200°C fan oven/425°F), gas
mark 7. Melt the butter in a pan and stir in the dried fruit,
sugar and spice.
2 On a lightly floured worksurface, roll out the pastry to a
2mm (⅛ inch) thickness. Cut out eight 12cm (5 inch) circles.
3 Place a spoonful of the fruit mixture in the centre of each
circle. Dampen the edges of the pastry with water and draw
into the centre, sealing well.
4 Turn over and flatten gently into a round with a rolling pin.
Whisk the egg white with a fork until frothy. Brush the tops of
the cakes with egg white and sprinkle with sugar. Make
3 diagonal cuts across each cake.
5 Bake in the oven for 15 minutes until lightly golden and
eat warm.

Cakes

Surely, there is a cake to suit every mood, palate and occasion? A slice of featherlight Victoria sponge filled with tangy raspberry jam for teatime, a slab of hearty fruit cake after a bracing winter walk or a dainty slice of Swiss roll at an outdoor summer spread will always please. If it's homemade, so much the better. Simplicity and good-quality ingredients are the key to all the best traditional country cakes, with ornate decoration and fanciful confections saved for special occasions. If you've never attempted to make a cake before, don't be nervous. Take your time, get everything ready, and always read the recipe through at least twice before starting. It really does matter. Take pleasure in the process from the measuring to the whisking and that care will result in a delicious cake. Don't rush and make sure to measure accurately. Even if it sinks in the middle at your first go or looks slightly overdone, a swirl of lightly whipped cream and a scattering of fresh fruit will hide any mistakes – call it a pudding and no one will be any the wiser. I guarantee it will taste better than anything shop-bought because it's made with fresh ingredients and lovingly prepared.

INGREDIENTS

The finer the raw ingredients, the more delicious the cake will be, therefore use quality butter and flour, unrefined sugars and free-range eggs wherever possible. **Fat** keeps a cake tender and imparts richness and flavour: **butter** produces the finest taste; **vegetable oil** gives a close, dense texture, moist crumb and good keeping qualities; **vegetable shortening** is flavourless but gives a fine texture. **Sugar** sweetens a cake and also helps to keep it tender. **Caster sugar** is the most suitable for cake making as it can be easily creamed with butter to incorporate extra air for rising. With their caramel flavours, **darker sugars** are best used for melting-method cakes, such as gingerbread, or creaming-method fruit cakes cooked at lower temperatures. **Golden syrup**, **treacle**, **honey** and **molasses** may be used as sweetening ingredients but result in a denser, heavier cake because less air can be incorporated during beating.

Plain or self-raising **flour** is most commonly used. Never use high-gluten strong flour because it results in a tough, chewy cake. **Cornflour**, **potato flour** and **rice flour** add extra lightness. **Eggs** give flavour and colour and should be used at room temperature to make them easier to incorporate into the creamed butter and sugar. Cold eggs can be quickly brought up to temperature in a bowl of warm water for a few minutes. Duck eggs are also suitable for baking and add extra flavour due to the richness of their yolks. Chemical raising agents, such as **bicarbonate of soda** and **baking powder**, can also be used to help cakes to rise and tend to be included when eggs are added whole rather than separated into yolks and beaten whites. **Bicarbonate of soda** works with acid ingredients, such as vinegar, molasses, yogurt, soured cream and buttermilk, to produce carbon dioxide that expands and helps a cake to rise. A pinch of **salt** gives depth of flavour to any sweet mixture.

EQUIPMENT

For successful cake making a selection of **good-quality bakeware** is vital. Always use the size of baking tin specified in the recipe as it affects cooking times and the thickness/shape of the cake. A **springform tin** is useful for delicate cakes that need careful unmoulding. **Silicone bakeware** has the advantage of being rust-proof and dishwasher-friendly. A lining of lightly greased **baking parchment** helps stop delicate cakes sticking and provides protection against oven heat during long cooking times. The correct oven temperature is important so it is worth investing in an **oven thermometer**. Other essential equipment includes a **sieve** for sifting flour, a **wooden spoon or electric hand-beaters** for beating and **wire racks** for cooling. A **free-standing mixer** is useful but not necessary.

A BIT OF TECHNIQUE

• Cakes containing a high proportion of butter (half or more to the weight of flour) are made with the **creaming method**. Cream (beat) softened butter and sugar with a wooden spoon or electric hand-beaters until soft, fluffy and lighter in colour. It enables eggs to be beaten in easily and adds more air to aid rise. Suitable for fruit cakes, layered cakes or loaf cakes. See the Classic Victoria Sandwich (page 42), Dundee Cake (page 43), Chocolate Butterfly Cakes (page 44), Lavender and Lemon Madeira Cake (page 45), Chocolate and Banana Loaf (page 52) and the Spiced Carrot Cake (page 53).

• Cakes containing relatively little butter in proportion to flour are made with the **rubbing-in method**: rub fat into the flour to distribute it evenly. A light touch, as with pastry, is needed to avoid producing a tough cake. These cakes are usually egg-free and leavening comes from chemical agents such as bicarbonate of soda, activated by an acid ingredient. See the Wholemeal Scones (page 50) and Vinegar Cake (page 50).

• Feather-light **whisked** cakes rely on the whisking process creating air in the batter while moisture in the eggs and butter converts to steam that expands in the oven. Make them in two ways: whisk whole eggs with sugar over low heat until thick enough to leave a ribbon trail (this gives a softer textured cake); or beat yolks over heat, then fold in flour and whisked egg whites. See the Vanilla and Raspberry Swiss Roll (page 47).

• **Melting method** cakes are the easiest to make: melt fat and sugar together, then stir in eggs and liquid before beating in dry ingredients. Put in the oven as soon as the wet ingredients activate the raising agent. See the Sticky Gingerbread Loaf (page 48) and Honey and Almond Cake (page 49).

Classic Victoria sandwich

Once you've mastered this basic recipe, vary the filling to suit the occasion: jams and curds for afternoon teas or a fresh fruit compote folded into freshly whipped cream for a special summer party.

PREPARATION **25 MINUTES**
COOKING **25 MINUTES**

Makes 1 x 20cm (8 inch) cake
225g (7½oz) unsalted butter, very soft, plus extra for greasing
225g (7½oz) caster sugar, plus extra for dusting
a pinch of salt
4 medium eggs, beaten
225g (7½oz) self-raising flour, sifted
1–2 tablespoons milk (optional)
3 tablespoons raspberry jam

1 Preheat the oven to 180°C (160°C fan oven/350°F), gas mark 4. Lightly grease two 20cm (8 inch) sandwich tins. Line each base with a circle of baking parchment.
2 Put the butter and sugar in a bowl with a pinch of salt and beat with a wooden spoon or electric hand-beaters until soft, fluffy and paler in colour. Add the eggs a little at a time whilst still stirring or with the beaters constantly running, beating well after each addition. If the mixture starts to curdle, beat in 1 tablespoon of the flour.
3 With a large metal spoon, gently fold in the flour, adding, if necessary, enough of the milk to bring the mixture to dropping consistency.
4 Divide the mixture between the 2 sandwich tins and bake in the oven for 25 minutes until risen and golden. The tops should spring back when lightly pressed. Remove from the oven and allow to cool for a few minutes before turning out of the tins onto wire racks and peeling away the paper.
5 Leave to cool completely, then sandwich the cakes together with jam. Dust the top with caster sugar. Store in an airtight container for up to 5 days.

Dundee cake

A light fruit cake characterized by the concentric circles of almonds. It will improve with keeping for a few days.

PREPARATION **35 MINUTES**
COOKING **2–2½ HOURS**

Makes 1 x 20cm (8 inch) cake
225g (7½oz) butter, softened, plus extra
  for greasing
225g (7½oz) caster sugar
grated zest of 1 lemon
grated zest of 1 orange
a pinch of salt
4 medium eggs, beaten
65g (2½oz) ground almonds
300g (10oz) plain flour, sifted
1 teaspoon baking powder
4 tablespoons milk
250g (8oz) currants
250g (8oz) sultanas
250g (8oz) raisins
75g (3oz) candied peel
125g (4oz) glacé cherries
75g (3oz) whole blanched almonds

1 Preheat the oven to 150°C (130°C fan oven/300°F), gas mark 2. Lightly grease a deep 20cm (8 inch) cake tin and line the base and sides with baking parchment.
2 Put the butter, sugar and zest in a bowl with a pinch of salt and beat with a wooden spoon or electric hand-beaters until soft, fluffy and paler in colour. Add the eggs a little at a time whilst still stirring or with the beaters constantly running, beating well after each addition. If the mixture starts to curdle, beat in 1 tablespoon of the flour.
3 With a large metal spoon, carefully fold in the ground almonds, followed by the flour and the baking powder. Fold in the milk and the fruit.
4 Turn the mixture into the prepared tin and level the surface. Arrange the almonds in concentric circles on the top. Bake in the oven for 2–2½ hours until a skewer inserted into the centre comes out clean. Cover the top with baking parchment or foil if it starts to overbrown during the cooking time. Remove from the oven and leave to cool in the tin set on a wire rack. Store in an airtight container for up to 1 week.

Chocolate butterfly cakes

Smaller and more delicate sweet morsels than a cupcake, they're a welcome addition to a traditional afternoon tea. Replace the filling with whipped cream and soft fruit for a special occasion.

1 Preheat the oven to 200°C (180°C fan oven/400°F), gas mark 6. Place 24 paper cake cases into two 12-hole bun trays.
2 Replacing 2 tablespoons of the flour with the cocoa powder, make one batch of Victoria sandwich mixture.
3 Divide the mixture between the paper cake cases (about three-quarters full) and bake in the oven for 10–15 minutes. Cool on a wire rack.
4 Meanwhile, make the buttercream. Using electric hand-beaters, soften the butter with the vanilla extract, then gradually add the icing sugar and cocoa powder until well blended.

5 Cut a shallow circle from the top of each cake and cut this shape in half to make 'wings'. Fit a piping bag with a large nozzle, fill with the buttercream and pipe a swirl into the centre of each cake. Arrange the 'wings' rounded side down and dust with icing sugar. Store in an airtight container for up to 5 days.

Variations

• Add 1 teaspoon grated lemon or orange zest to the plain sponge mixture.
• For a citrus buttercream, omit the cocoa powder and add 1–2 teaspoons lemon or orange juice to taste.

PREPARATION **35 MINUTES**
COOKING **10–15 MINUTES**

Makes 24
1 quantity Classic Victoria Sandwich mixture (see page 42)
2 tablespoons cocoa powder, sifted
icing sugar, for dusting

FOR THE BUTTERCREAM ICING
110g (3½oz) unsalted butter, softened
a few drops of vanilla extract
225g (7½oz) icing sugar, sifted
1 tablespoon cocoa powder, sifted

Lavender and lemon Madeira cake

Simply omit the lavender for a classic version of this cake.

PREPARATION **35 MINUTES**
COOKING **1¼ HOURS**

Makes 1 x 17cm (6½ inch) cake
175g (6oz) unsalted butter, softened, plus extra for greasing
175g (6oz) lavender sugar (see page 96)
grated zest and juice of 1 lemon
a pinch of salt
3 medium eggs, beaten
115g (3½oz) self-raising flour
55g (2¼oz) ground almonds
milk (optional)

FOR THE ICING
2 sprigs fresh or dried lavender
175g (6oz) icing sugar, sifted
1 tablespoon lemon juice

1 Lightly grease a 17cm (6½ inch) tin and line the base with a circle of baking parchment. Preheat the oven to 160°C (140°C fan oven/325°F), gas mark 3.
2 Put the butter and sugar in a bowl with the lemon zest and salt and beat with a wooden spoon or electric hand-beaters until soft, fluffy and paler in colour. Add the eggs a little at a time whilst still stirring or with the beaters constantly running, beating well after each addition. If the mixture starts to curdle, beat in 1 tablespoon of flour. Add the lemon juice.
3 With a large metal spoon, gently fold in the flour and almonds, adding, if necessary, a drop of milk to bring the mixture to dropping consistency. Spoon into the cake tin and bake in the oven for 1¼ hours until risen and golden.

The top should spring back when lightly pressed with a finger. Remove from the oven and allow to cool for a few minutes before turning out of the tin onto a wire rack and peeling away the paper.
4 Meanwhile, make the icing. Strip the lavender flowers from their stalks if using fresh and put into a bowl with the rest of the icing ingredients. Mix until smooth – the mixture should thickly coat the back of a spoon. If necessary, add warm water drop by drop until the desired consistency is achieved.
5 When the cake is completely cold, pour over the icing and leave to set before serving. Decorate with fresh lavender sprigs if you like. Store in an airtight container for up to 5 days.

Vanilla and raspberry Swiss roll

The filling could be replaced with a few tablespoons of jam or fruit compote, or make a chocolate version by swapping half of the flour for cocoa powder.

1 Preheat the oven to 220°C (200°C fan oven/425°F), gas mark 7. Grease a 33 x 23cm (13 x 9 inch) Swiss roll tin and line the base with greased baking parchment. Dust with caster sugar, then flour. Tap out the excess.
2 To make the Swiss roll, whisk the eggs and 100g (3½oz) of the sugar in a large bowl until the mixture is thick and pale – the whisk should leave a trail for a few seconds when lifted out.
3 Using a large metal spoon, gently but quickly fold the flour and baking powder into the mixture using a figure of eight movement.
4 Pour the mixture into the tin, gently knocking out any flour pockets with the spoon if necessary. Level the mixture, spreading it out into the corners. Bake for 5–6 minutes until golden and the cake shrinks from the edges of the tin.
5 Meanwhile, put a piece of baking parchment slightly larger than the cake on the worksurface. Sprinkle with the remaining caster sugar.
6 Turn the cake out onto the sugared paper. Remove the tin and carefully peel away the paper. Trim the edges of the cake to neaten and make a light score mark 2.5cm (1 inch) in from one short edge. Using the paper under the cake to help, roll up the cake tightly from the scored short end. Leave it rolled up while it cools.
7 To make the filling, lightly whip the cream with the vanilla extract and icing sugar until it just holds its shape. Gently fold in the raspberries.
8 To assemble the Swiss roll, unroll the sponge and spread with the cream mixture. Re-roll tightly and put on a serving plate or board. Cut into slices to serve and consume within 3 days.

PREPARATION **35 MINUTES**
COOKING **ABOUT 30 MINUTES**

Makes 1 x 23cm (9 inch) Swiss roll
butter, for greasing
160g (5½oz) caster sugar, plus extra for dusting
50g (2oz) plain flour, sifted, plus extra for dusting
3 medium eggs
1 teaspoon baking powder

FOR THE FILLING
200ml (7fl oz) double cream
1 teaspoon vanilla extract
2 tablespoons icing sugar, sifted
150g (5oz) fresh raspberries

Sticky gingerbread loaf

This gingerbread improves with age, becoming more deliciously sticky after a few days. Wrap in greaseproof paper and store in an airtight tin.

PREPARATION **25 MINUTES**
COOKING **ABOUT 1 HOUR**

Makes 1 x 900g (1 ¾lb) loaf cake
100g (3½oz) butter, plus extra for
  greasing
100g (3½oz) soft dark brown sugar
100g (3½oz) black treacle
120ml (4fl oz) milk
140g (4½oz) plain flour
1 level teaspoon ground ginger
1 level teaspoon ground cinnamon
1 level teaspoon bicarbonate of soda
1 medium egg, beaten
2 balls stem ginger, roughly chopped,
  plus 2 tablespoons of the syrup

1 Preheat the oven to 150°C (130°C fan oven/300°F), gas mark 2. Lightly grease a 900g (1¾lb) loaf tin and line the base and sides with baking parchment.

2 Melt the butter, sugar and treacle in a saucepan over a low heat until the sugar is dissolved. Stir in the milk and allow to cool a little.

3 Sift together the flour, spices and bicarbonate of soda. Quickly beat into the melted butter mixture along with the egg, stem ginger and syrup, ensuring there are no pockets of flour, and turn into the prepared loaf tin.

4 Bake in the oven for about 1 hour — cover the top with a piece of baking parchment if it starts to overbrown. The gingerbread is cooked when a skewer inserted in the centre comes out clean. Remove from the oven and leave to cool on a wire rack.

Honey and almond cake

Experiment with different honey for subtle flavour changes.

PREPARATION **35 MINUTES** —
COOKING **1¼ HOURS**

Makes 1 x 20cm (8 inch) cake
75g (3oz) butter, plus extra for greasing
225ml (7½fl oz) clear orange blossom honey, plus 3 tablespoons, to finish
300g (10oz) plain wholemeal flour
50g (2oz) ground almonds
1 teaspoon mixed spice
1 teaspoon bicarbonate of soda
3 medium eggs, beaten
3 tablespoons milk
grated zest of 1 orange
25g (1oz) flaked almonds, to decorate

1 Preheat the oven to 160°C (140°C fan oven/325°F), gas mark 3. Lightly grease and line the base and sides of a 20cm (8 inch) square cake tin. Put the honey and butter in a saucepan and heat gently to melt together. Cool slightly.

2 Sift the flour, almonds, spice and bicarbonate of soda into a large bowl.

3 Stir the eggs, milk and orange zest into the honey. Make a well in the centre of the flour and pour in the honey mixture. Quickly blend the ingredients together, then pour into the prepared tin. Sprinkle over the almonds and bake for 1¼ hours until a skewer inserted into the centre comes out clean.

4 While the cake is still hot, prick with a skewer and drizzle over the honey. Leave to cool in the tin for 10 minutes, then turn out onto a wire rack. Store in an airtight container for up to 1 week.

Wholemeal scones

Scones are best eaten on the day they're made and are delicious warm from the oven.

PREPARATION **15 MINUTES**
COOKING **12–15 MINUTES**

Makes 6–8
125g (4oz) self-raising white flour
125g (4oz) self-raising wholemeal flour
1 teaspoon baking powder
a pinch of salt
40g (1½oz) cold unsalted butter, diced, plus extra for greasing
150ml (¼ pint) milk or buttermilk
beaten egg, to glaze
butter, cream or jam, to serve

1 Preheat the oven to 220°C (200°C fan oven/425°F), gas mark 7. Sift the flours and baking powder into a large bowl with the salt. Rub in the butter until the mixture resembles fine breadcrumbs. Alternatively, blitz the mixture in a food processor, then transfer to a bowl.
2 Using a flat-bladed table knife, gradually work in enough milk to form a soft, but not too sticky dough.
3 Turn onto a lightly floured worksurface and knead briefly to bring the dough together – overhandling will make the scones tough. Lightly press out to a 2.5cm (1 inch) thickness and cut out rounds with a 6cm (2½ inch) cutter. Re-roll the trimmings if you like, although they won't be quite as light.
4 Put the scones on a lightly greased baking tray, spaced well apart, and brush the tops with the egg – try not to let the egg run down the sides as it will inhibit the scones rising. Bake for 12–15 minutes until well risen and golden. Transfer to a wire rack to cool. Serve warm or cold, split in half and spread with butter or cream and jam.

Variations

• **Plain:** replace the wholemeal flour with the same amount of white self-raising flour.
• **Fruit:** Add 100g (3½oz) raisins and 1 tablespoon caster sugar to the rubbed in mixture before adding the milk.
• **Cheese:** Add 100g (3½oz) grated strong Cheddar and a pinch each of cayenne pepper and English mustard powder after the butter is rubbed in.

Vinegar cake

This egg-free cake has a lighter texture than most fruit cakes and you won't be able to detect the vinegar! It's particularly good served with a slice of Wensleydale cheese.

PREPARATION **30 MINUTES**
COOKING **2 HOURS**

Makes 1 x 23cm (9 inch) cake
225g (7½oz) butter, diced, plus extra for greasing
450g (14½oz) plain white flour, sifted
225g (7½oz) soft light brown sugar
175g (6 oz) sultanas
125g (4oz) dried apricots, chopped
150g (5oz) dried cranberries
1 teaspoon bicarbonate of soda
300ml (½ pint) milk
3 tablespoons malt or distilled vinegar

1 Preheat the oven to 200°C (180°C fan oven/400°F), gas mark 6. Lightly grease and line the base and sides of a deep 23cm (9 inch) cake tin with baking parchment.
2 Rub the butter into the flour until the mixture resembles fine breadcrumbs. Stir in the sugar and dried fruit.
3 Mix together the remaining ingredients in a separate bowl. Stir immediately into the flour mixture until combined.
4 Pour into the prepared cake tin and bake in the oven for 30 minutes. Turn down the oven temperature to 160°C (140°C fan oven/325°F), gas mark 3 and bake for another 1½ hours until a skewer inserted into the centre of the cake comes out clean. If the top starts to overbrown, cover with a piece of foil.
5 Leave to cool in the tin for 20 minutes, then turn out onto a wire rack to cool completely. Store in an airtight container for up to 1 week.

Chocolate and banana loaf

This is also good when made with a flavoured chocolate, such as ginger, or butterscotch.

PREPARATION **35 MINUTES**
COOKING **45–50 MINUTES**

Makes 1 x 900g (1¾lb) loaf cake
115g (3½oz) butter, melted and cooled, plus extra for greasing
300g (10oz) plain flour
40g (1½oz) cocoa powder
4 teaspoons baking powder
1 teaspoon bicarbonate of soda
3 large bananas, about 300g (10oz) peeled weight, mashed
150g (5oz) caster sugar
3 medium eggs, beaten
175g (6oz) plain chocolate, chopped

1 Preheat the oven to 190°C (170°C fan oven/375°F), gas mark 5. Lightly grease and line a 900g (1¾lb) loaf tin. Sift the flour, cocoa powder, baking powder and bicarbonate of soda in a large bowl.
2 Stir together the bananas, sugar, eggs and butter. Fold in the flour, followed by the chocolate.

3 Turn into the prepared tin, smooth the top and bake in the oven for 45–50 minutes until a skewer inserted into the centre comes out clean. Leave to cool in the tin for 5 minutes before turning out onto a wire rack. Store in an airtight container for up to 1 week.

Spiced carrot cake

Once iced, this cake will keep in the fridge for up to 5 days.

PREPARATION 30 MINUTES
COOKING 50–60 MINUTES

Makes 21 pieces

175g (6oz) self-raising white flour, sifted
100g (3½oz) self-raising wholemeal
  flour, sifted
350g (11½oz) caster sugar
2 teaspoons baking powder
75g (3oz) walnuts, roughly chopped
3 teaspoons mixed spice
2 teaspoons ground ginger
4 medium eggs
300ml (½ pint) sunflower oil
1 teaspoon vanilla extract
275g (9oz) carrots, grated

FOR THE ICING

100g (3½oz) unsalted butter, softened
100g (3½oz) icing sugar, sifted
400g (13oz) cream cheese
1 tablespoon runny honey, plus extra
  for drizzling
juice of half a lemon

1 Preheat the oven to 180°C (160°C fan oven/400°F), gas mark 4. Lightly grease and line a 30 x 23cm (12 x 9 inch) tin with baking parchment.
2 Put all of the dry ingredients into a large bowl. Stir to combine. Beat the eggs into the oil with the vanilla extract.
3 Make a well in the centre of the flour and pour in the oil along with the carrots.

Mix together quickly, then pour into the prepared tin.
4 Bake for 50–60 minutes until risen and golden. Cool in the tin for 10 minutes, then turn onto a wire rack.
5 Beat together the icing ingredients until smooth and chill until thickened. Spread the icing on the cake and drizzle with honey before serving.

Biscuits and traybakes

It should be a rule that every country kitchen owns a slightly battered tin brimming with homemade biscuits or cookies ready to offer with coffee to unexpected guests or simply for the pure enjoyment of your own elevenses. Biscuit making is one of the easiest of the baking arts to master but no less pleasurable for that. Half an hour or so in the kitchen is all it takes to produce a batch of tempting delights: crumbly shortbread; chunky cookies; oatcakes to enjoy with cheese; sweet or savoury; crunchy or gooey; plain or lavish. The variety is endless but the necessary basic ingredients are few. A sprinkling of nuts or chocolate are welcome embellishments, but even the plainest recipe will delight when enjoyed with a nice cup of tea and a sit down…

INGREDIENTS

A delicious biscuit can be created with just a few simple storecupboard ingredients, like **butter**, **sugar**, **flour** and **eggs**. But once that basic recipe is mastered, a whole range of ingredients may be added to create endless flavour and texture combinations. **Rice flour** produces a lighter, more crumbly texture; **semolina** gives crunch, while **ground almonds** or **hazelnuts** impart a delicate nuttiness. **Ground spices** bring warmth and depth; darker, **unrefined sugars** colour and give a fuller flavour; cocoa powder or **chocolate chips** add delightful indulgence. **Honey**, **treacle** and **molasses** give extra sweetness and depth of flavour and marry very well with aromatic spices, like **cinnamon**, **nutmeg** and **ginger**. Firm syrup doughs, such as **gingerbread**, are robust enough to roll into large sheets suitable for baking and making into gingerbread houses. **Flavoured sugars**, such as lavender, vanilla and cinnamon, come into their own, while grated **citrus zest** is a welcome but subtle addition. **Oats**, **wheatgerm** and **wholemeal** flours give a healthy, nutty dimension to savoury biscuits. For a pleasing contrasting texture, crunchy biscuits can be sandwiched with creamy, flavoured **buttercreams**, or decorated with **glacé** or **royal icing**.

EQUIPMENT

Little is needed in the way of specialist equipment. A basic creamed biscuit mixture can be created with a **wooden spoon**, a **bowl** and a lot of **elbow grease**. However, **electric hand-beaters** or a **free-standing mixer** will make life easier and enable you to expand your repertoire quickly. Invest in flat and heavy, light-coloured **baking sheets**, which conduct heat more evenly. A **wire rack** is essential for cooling biscuits and stops the bottoms becoming soggy. A **rolling pin**, **metal palette knife** and **pastry brush** are useful. A **piping bag** will allow you to create fanciful shapes.

Biscuit cutters come in many shapes and sizes, from plain and fluted to festive and themed, such as animals or letters. Invest in them as and when you please; they are not essential. For simple rounds, the rim of a glass is sufficient for stamping out shapes. Very precise shapes can be achieved with a **biscuit press**: it comprises a metal cylinder with interchangeable discs, which is filled with creamed dough mixture. The mixture is pressed through the holes in the disc to make a pattern. However, the biscuits tend to be small and are more suitable for serving as petit fours.

Baking parchment gives excellent anti-sticking properties and is best for lining baking sheets when making biscuits with a high sugar content (don't use greaseproof paper as they're more likely to stick). Alternatively, rolls of **silicone liners** are available from good cookshops, which can be cut to the size of your baking sheets, washed and used again and again.

Dedicated biscuit makers should rummage in antique and vintage shops and markets for **carved wooden rolling pins**, known in Germany as *springerle*. A tradition in many northern European countries and especially used at Christmas time, they are carved with elaborate designs and rolled across biscuit dough to imprint a pattern before baking.

A BIT OF TECHNIQUE

- Like pastry making, a light touch is essential when rubbing in fat, working in flour or rolling out dough to avoid tough or heavy biscuits.
- Flour worksurfaces sparingly when rolling as too much will make biscuits over-dry. Only roll dough out once for the same reason.
- Avoid over-beating a creamed mixture when adding egg – too much air produces biscuits with a cake-like texture.
- If the mixture over-spreads during baking the proportion of fat or sugar is too high; bake a test biscuit first if in doubt.
- Once cooked, leave the biscuits on the baking sheet for 1–2 minutes until firm enough to transfer to a wire rack to cool completely before transferring to an airtight tin.
- Don't store biscuits in the same tins as cake because they will soften and taste stale. Interleave sticky biscuits with sheets of greaseproof paper or waxed paper.
- Most biscuits will last for about 5 days in an airtight container after baking; biscuits high in fat, such as shortbread or those with a low moisture content, such as biscotti, will keep for up to 1 month. Alternatively, freeze, ensuring they are well wrapped, for up to 1 month.
- Slightly stale biscuits can be revived for 5 minutes in the oven at 150°C (130°C fan oven/300°F), gas mark 2.

From left to right:
Vanilla shortbread (see page 61);
Peanut butter and raisin cookies (see page 60);
Refrigerator cookies (see page 61);
and Almond macaroons (see page 60).

Peanut butter and raisin cookies

A cookie more suitable for adult tastes, combining sweet raisins and savoury peanut butter: use an unsweetened version if you prefer a less sweet biscuit.

PREPARATION **20 MINUTES**
COOKING **15 MINUTES**

Makes 12 cookies
125g (4oz) unsalted butter, softened,
  plus extra for greasing
150g (5oz) caster sugar
1 medium egg
125g (4oz) crunchy peanut butter
150g (5oz) plain flour, sifted
½ teaspoon baking powder
150g (5oz) raisins

1 Preheat the oven to 190°C (170°C fan oven/375°F), gas mark 5 and lightly grease 2 baking sheets.
2 Cream together the butter and sugar until light and fluffy. Beat in the egg until combined, followed by the peanut butter.
3 Add the flour and baking powder and stir to combine. Add the raisins.
4 Drop dessertspoons of the mixture onto the baking sheets, spacing well apart to allow for spreading. Bake in the oven for 15 minutes. Leave to cool on the baking sheets for 2 minutes, then transfer to a wire rack to cool completely. Store in an airtight container for up to 5 days.

Almond macaroons

Macaroons are traditionally made on rice paper, but if it is difficult to get hold of, you can line baking sheets with silicone paper as an alternative.

PREPARATION **15 MINUTES**
COOKING **20–25 MINUTES**

Makes 16 macaroons
8 whole blanched almonds
2 large egg whites
125g (4oz) ground almonds
175g (6oz) caster sugar
25g (1oz) rice flour
¼ teaspoon almond extract

1 Preheat the oven to 160°C (140°C fan oven/325°F), gas mark 3. Line 2 baking sheets with rice or silicone paper. Split the almonds in half lengthways.
2 Whisk the egg whites in a large bowl until they are forming soft peaks.
3 Fold in the ground almonds, caster sugar, rice flour and almond extract.
4 Put teaspoons of the mixture onto the baking sheet and press down slightly with the back of a spoon. Place an almond half in the centre. Bake in the oven for 20–25 minutes until lightly golden. Leave on the baking sheet for 2 minutes to set, then transfer to a wire rack to cool. Cut around the rice paper, if using, before storing in an airtight container for up to 5 days.

Vanilla shortbread

Don't panic if the mixture seems too crumbly, pressing it on the baking sheet will ensure it sticks together for baking.

PREPARATION **20 MINUTES**
COOKING **20–30 MINUTES**

Makes 6–8 pieces
125g (4oz) unsalted butter, diced, plus extra for greasing
125g (4oz) plain flour
60g (2½oz) rice flour
60g (2½oz) vanilla sugar (see below)

1 Preheat the oven to 180°C (160°C fan oven/350°F), gas mark 4 and lightly grease a baking sheet.
2 Sift both flours into a large bowl and stir in the sugar. Rub in the butter until the mixture is crumbly and the fat is evenly distributed.
3 Lightly knead the mixture into a ball – don't use any liquid as the moisture from the butter should be sufficient.
4 Dust the worksurface with rice flour and press the ball into a 20cm (8 inch) round (or press into a shortbread mould). Crimp the edges with your fingers, then transfer to the baking sheet. Chill for 30 minutes.
5 Score the surface into wedge-shaped portions, then prick all over with a fork. Bake in the oven for 20–30 minutes until the shortbread feels firm to the touch and is lightly golden in colour. Leave to set for a few minutes before transferring to a wire rack to cool. When cold, slice into wedges using the score marks as your guide. Store in an airtight container for up to 1 week.

Tip
Save used vanilla pods from making ice cream or custard to create your own vanilla sugar. Rinse and dry the empty pods and bury 1 or 2 split vanilla pods in a large jar of caster sugar. Leave to infuse for 2 weeks before using.

Refrigerator cookies

The dough can be frozen as a log or kept in the fridge for up to 2 weeks and slices cut and baked when needed.

PREPARATION **20 MINUTES**
COOKING **8–10 MINUTES**

Makes 30–40 cookies
125g (4oz) unsalted butter, softened, plus extra for greasing
125g (4oz) caster sugar
1 medium egg
1 teaspoon vanilla extract
250g (8oz) plain flour, sifted
¼ teaspoon baking powder
a pinch of salt
1½ tablespoons cocoa powder
1 egg white, lightly beaten with a fork

1 Cream together the butter and sugar until light and fluffy. Beat in the egg and vanilla extract until combined.
2 Combine the flour, baking powder and salt with the butter mixture using a wooden spoon. Bring together with your hands if it becomes too stiff to work with the spoon.
3 Divide the mixture into 2 portions and work the cocoa powder into one half. Wrap each portion in cling film and chill for 30 minutes.
4 Lightly flour the worksurface and roll out each piece of dough into a rectangle 2mm (1/10 inch) thick. Trim to make both rectangles the same size.
5 Brush the light dough with egg white and place the dark dough on top. Brush the top with more egg white. Starting at one of the long sides, roll both layers of the dough together into a long sausage shape. Wrap in cling film and chill until firm.
6 Preheat the oven to 190°C (170°C fan oven/375°F), gas mark 5 and lightly grease 2 baking sheets. Cut the dough into 5mm (¼ inch) slices, place them on the greased baking sheets, leaving at least 5cm (2 inches) between each one to allow for spreading. Bake in the oven for 8–10 minutes until lightly golden and firm to the touch. Leave to cool on the baking sheets for 2 minutes, then transfer to a wire rack to cool completely. Store in an airtight container for up to 5 days.

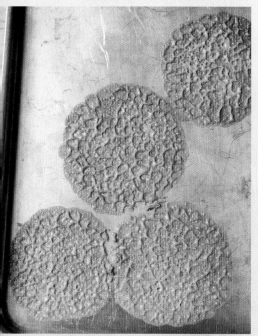

Brandy snaps

Don't be tempted to cook too many biscuits at once as they will harden before you have time to mould them around the wooden spoons.

PREPARATION **20 MINUTES**
COOKING **30 MINUTES**

Makes 12–15 brandy snaps
75g (3oz) unsalted butter, plus extra for greasing
flavourless oil, for greasing
75g (3oz) caster sugar
3 tablespoons golden syrup
75g (3oz) plain flour
1 teaspoon ground ginger
2 tablespoons brandy
juice of half a lemon
cream, to serve (optional)

1 Preheat the oven to 190°C (170°C fan oven/375°F), gas mark 5 and lightly grease 2 baking sheets. Lightly oil the handles of 2–3 wooden spoons.
2 Melt the butter, sugar and golden syrup in a pan set over a low heat until combined. Cool for a few minutes.
3 Sift together the flour and ground ginger, then beat into the butter mixture with the brandy and lemon juice.
4 Put tablespoons of the mixture onto the baking sheets, spacing well apart to allow for spreading. You will need to bake the mixture in batches. Bake in the oven for 8–10 minutes until golden brown with a lacy texture.
5 Leave the brandy snaps on the baking sheet for 10 seconds or so to firm up slightly. Working quickly, remove the brandy snaps with a palette knife and roll them around the wooden spoon handles. Transfer to a wire rack to cool and remove from the spoons as soon as they are set. If the brandy snaps harden before you have time to roll them, pop them back in the oven for a few seconds to re-soften.
6 Store in an airtight container for several days. Fill with lightly whipped cream if you like, just before serving.

Florentines

A touch of spice adds a seasonal flavour to these Florentines.

PREPARATION **30 MINUTES**
COOKING **30 MINUTES**

Makes about 50 florentines
55g (2¼oz) unsalted butter
90ml (6 tablespoons) double cream
110g (3½oz) golden granulated sugar
110g (3½oz) flaked toasted almonds
110g (3½oz) chopped toasted hazelnuts
110g (3½oz) glacé cherries, chopped
55g (2¼oz) candied orange peel, finely chopped
finely grated tangerine zest
½ teaspoon ground cinnamon
½ nutmeg, grated
55g (2¼oz) plain flour
¼ teaspoon salt
250g (8oz) dark chocolate

1 Preheat the oven to 180°C (160°C fan oven/350°F), gas mark 4. Line 2 or more baking sheets with baking parchment, or use non-stick trays or silicone liners.
2 Put the butter, cream and sugar in a heavy-based pan and heat slowly, stirring until the sugar dissolves. Bring the mixture to the boil, then remove the pan from the heat and stir in the almonds, hazelnuts, cherries, candied peel, tangerine zest, cinnamon, nutmeg, flour and salt.
3 Drop teaspoons of the mixture onto the prepared trays, spacing them well apart to allow for spreading. Use a wet knife to flatten each one, then bake in the oven for 8–10 minutes, or until they begin to brown at the edges. While still warm, transfer to a wire rack and leave to cool.
4 Break the chocolate into a large bowl and set it over a small pan of water that has just boiled and been taken off the heat. Let the chocolate warm slowly, stirring until it is fully melted. Alternatively, melt it in a microwave. Spread the smooth underside of each florentine with the melted chocolate, then set them back on the racks, chocolate side up, and leave to harden.
5 When cold, store the florentines in an airtight container for 1–2 weeks.

Thyme oatcakes

Swap the thyme for rosemary or omit the herbs altogether if you prefer a plain biscuit. Perfect served with your favourite cheese and chutney.

PREPARATION **20 MINUTES PLUS STANDING**
COOKING **20–30 MINUTES**

Makes 16 oatcakes
150g (5oz) medium oatmeal, plus extra for rolling
1 teaspoon chopped thyme leaves
a pinch of salt
15g (½oz) butter or lard, diced
125ml (4fl oz) boiling water

1 Preheat the oven to 180°C (160°C fan oven/350°F), gas mark 4 and line 2 baking sheets with baking parchment.
2 Put the oatmeal in a bowl and stir in the thyme leaves with a pinch of salt.
3 Add the butter or lard to the boiling water. Once melted, stir this into the oatmeal and leave to stand for 5 minutes.
4 When cool enough to handle, bring the oatmeal together into a dough and knead briefly. Dust the worksurface with oatmeal and roll out to a 2mm (¹⁄₁₀ inch) thickness. Stamp out rounds with a 6cm (2½ inch) round cutter and transfer to the baking sheets. Bake in the oven for 20–30 minutes. Cool on a wire rack. Store in an airtight container for up to 1 week.

Fruit and mixed seed flapjacks

This simple traybake is easy to adapt with your favourite dried fruit and seeds – just keep the proportions the same.

PREPARATION **20 MINUTES**
COOKING **23–30 MINUTES**

Makes 24 flapjacks
175g (6oz) unsalted butter, plus extra for greasing
125g (4oz) golden caster sugar
50g (2oz) golden syrup
225g (7½oz) porridge oats
2 tablespoons plain flour
a pinch of ground ginger
a pinch of salt
125g (4oz) mixed dried fruit
50g (2oz) mixture of pumpkin, sunflower and sesame seeds

1 Preheat the oven to 190°C (170°C fan oven/375°F), gas mark 5. Grease and line a shallow 30 x 35cm (12 x 14 inch) baking tin or a tin that has sides that add up to the same measurements.
2 Melt the butter, sugar and golden syrup together in a pan set over a low heat. Mix together the oats, flour, ginger and salt. Stir into the butter mixture, then add the fruit and seeds.
3 Turn the mixture into the prepared tin and bake in the oven for 25–30 minutes until golden. Cut into squares in the tin while still warm. Store in an airtight container for up to 1 week.

Sweets

The frivolity of making sweets and chocolates always pleases me. It is food for sheer pleasure rather than an everyday necessity; their purpose is only to delight or reward. But, for me, most of the fun lies in making them, then wrapping in pretty boxes or vintage jars to give as presents. Having said that, sweet making does take some concentration and meticulous preparation. When dealing with boiling sugar syrups for fudge or boiled sweets, you must watch the thermometer like a hawk, while melting chocolate can easily seize if left unattended or stirred too vigorously. So take your time and enjoy the process and you'll be rewarded with bags of sweet joy.

Dark chocolate truffles (see page 72)

Barley sugar

Sweets don't get any more old-fashioned than barley sugar – a lemon-flavoured sugar syrup boiled to such a high temperature that it will be hard and brittle and a joy to eat when cold.

PREPARATION **5 MINUTES**
COOKING **20 MINUTES**

Makes about 450g (14½oz)
oil, for greasing
450g (14½oz) golden granulated sugar
150ml (¼ pint) water
1 unwaxed lemon
¼ teaspoon cream of tartar

1 Generously oil the worksurface or silicone sheet you will be pouring the molten sugar onto.

2 Put the sugar and water into a medium-sized pan over a low heat, stirring occasionally until the sugar has dissolved fully. Wash down any sugar crystals from the sides of the pan with a wet pastry brush. At the same time, pare the zest of the lemon in large pieces, without the white pith; squeeze and reserve the juice.

3 Add the lemon zest and cream of tartar to the syrup, raise the heat and boil it to 116°C (240°F). Add the lemon juice and continue boiling until the syrup reaches the hard-crack stage, 154°C (310°F). Remove the pan from the heat,

dip the base briefly in cold water, then pour the syrup out onto the prepared worksurface.

4 Allow the syrup to cool a little until it stiffens at the edges and begins to form a skin. Use an oiled palette knife to lift one edge of the hardening puddle and fold it into the centre. Fold over the opposite edge to cover the double layer, making a three-layered rectangle.

5 Working quickly, use oiled scissors to cut the barley sugar into narrow strips. Twist each into a curly stick and set aside on the oiled surface to harden completely.

6 Wrap each piece of barley sugar individually in waxed paper or cellophane and store in an airtight container.

Makes about 900g (1¾lb)

110g (3½oz) salted butter, plus extra
  for greasing
700g (1lb 7oz) golden granulated sugar
175ml (6fl oz) water
400g (13oz) tin sweetened condensed
  milk
½ teaspoon ground cardamom seeds

Cardamom fudge

The subtle flavouring of cardamom in this fudge makes it quite irresistible.

1 Butter or oil a 20 x 30cm (8 x 12 inch) non-stick tin.

2 Slowly heat the sugar in a heavy pan with the water, milk and butter until it is dissolved completely. Wash down any sugar crystals from the sides of the pan with a wet pastry brush.

3 Raise the heat, boil the syrup to the soft-ball stage (113°C (235°F) on a confectionery or sugar thermometer), remove the pan from the heat and dip the base in cold water.

4 Let the syrup rest for a minute or two, then, with a wooden spoon, stir in the cardamom. Continue stirring until the syrup starts to grain and stiffen, then pour into the prepared tin.

5 While warm, mark into squares, then cut into pieces when cold. Store in an airtight container, separated by greaseproof paper.

Dried fruit balls

Easy, quick and full of flavour and goodness, serve as petit fours with coffee.

Makes about 20 balls

100g (3½oz) dried apricots

100g (3½oz) mixed raisins, sultanas and currants

100g (3½oz) soft prunes, stoned

50g (2oz) sweetened dried cranberries

50g (2oz) shelled pistachios

finely grated zest of 1 unwaxed lemon

¼ teaspoon ground cinnamon

a pinch of ground cloves

up to 2 tablespoons each honey and ground almonds as needed

150g (5oz) granulated sugar

1 Work the apricots, raisin mixture, prunes, cranberries and pistachios through the finest blade of a mincer into a bowl. You can blitz in a blender or food processor but be careful not to overwork the mixture to a purée.

2 Sprinkle over the lemon zest, cinnamon and cloves. Mix well, adding a little honey if too dry, or a spoonful of ground almonds if too sticky.

3 Put the sugar in a shallow dish. Form small spoonfuls of the fruit mixture into balls by rolling them between your palms. Roll the balls in the sugar, then set in individual petit four paper cases. Decorate with dried fruit if you like. They can be eaten at once, or stored for 1 week or more in an airtight container.

Dark chocolate truffles

Give these truffles a fascinating whiff of smoke by adding a splash of an Islay malt whisky, such as Laphroaig. Alternatively, you could infuse the cream with black cardamom pods, which have a very different flavour from the more familiar green cardamoms – or both. Brandy or fruit liqueurs are other possible flavourings.

PREPARATION **10 MINUTES**
COOKING **15 MINUTES**

Makes about 24 truffles
100ml (3½fl oz) double cream
6 whole black cardamom pods
250g (8oz) dark chocolate
1 tablespoon Islay whisky
1 teaspoon vanilla extract
cocoa powder, for dusting

1 Heat the cream and cardamom pods in a small pan, or microwave until hot, but not boiling. Leave to infuse until lukewarm.

2 Break the chocolate into a large bowl and set it over a small pan of water that has just boiled and been taken off the heat. Let the chocolate warm slowly, stirring until it is fully melted. Alternatively, melt it in a microwave.

3 Strain the warm cream into the melted chocolate, stirring until smooth.

4 Let the mixture cool to room temperature before incorporating the whisky and vanilla extract and whisking the mixture until it lightens in colour and holds soft peaks. Chill for 10 minutes to firm before forming the truffles.

5 Sift a thick layer of cocoa powder onto a tray. Cover another with greaseproof paper. With 2 teaspoons, drop small, even-sized blobs of the mixture into the cocoa. Dust your fingers with cocoa, roll each blob into a ball, roll it in the cocoa and set it on the paper.

6 The truffles are ready to eat as they are, or can be rolled in chopped nuts or finely grated chocolate, or dipped in melted chocolate and decorated with gold leaf (see page 67 and Tip, below).

Tip
For a bit of festive sparkle, use gold leaf for decoration (you'll need loose, not transfer gold – available on the internet). Touch the thin gold sheets with a fine artist's brush – tiny pieces will stick to it and can be transferred to the truffles.

Makes about 600g (1lb 3oz)
4 unwaxed oranges
1.1 litres (1¾ pints) water
675g (1lb 6oz) granulated sugar

TO FINISH (OPTIONAL)
caster sugar, for dredging
melted dark chocolate

Candied peel

Candied peel takes several days to prepare but the flavour is incomparable to the commercial variety and keeps for several months in an airtight container.

1 Cut the oranges into quarters and remove the flesh. Put the peel into a large pan with the water. Bring to the boil then simmer very gently for about 1 hour until the peel is tender but keeps its shape.

2 Reserve 600ml (1 pint) of the cooking liquid. Drain the peel and put in a non-metallic bowl.

3 Dissolve 450g (14½oz) of the sugar in a pan with the reserved cooking liquid. When all the sugar is dissolved, turn up the heat and boil for 1 minute. Pour over the peel, cover and leave to stand for 24 hours.

4 The next day, strain the liquid into a pan and add the remaining sugar. Dissolve and boil as in step 3. Pour over the peel, cover and leave to stand for another 24 hours.

5 On day 3, put the peel and syrup into a heavy-based pan and bring to the boil. Simmer for 30–60 minutes until the pith is transparent – this will depend on the thickness of the peel. Transfer to a bowl, cover and leave the peel to stand in the liquid for 4 days.

6 On day 7, drain and leave the peel on a wire rack in a cool, dry place for 1 week until no longer sticky.

7 To make a pleasing gift, the peel can be cut into slices and dusted with caster sugar while still slightly tacky or the ends dipped into melted chocolate and left to set.

8 Layer the peel between sheets of waxed paper. Alternatively, store in an airtight container for several months and use when needed in baking.

Dairy

The dairy products we take for granted today are often the result of happy accidents in the past – tweaked by generations of **dairymaids and farmers' wives** into constancy by experience handed down. But, with a little technical help, you can achieve satisfying results in your own kitchen too. The small but **pleasurable miracles** that convert fresh cream into **golden butter** and milk into **soft, yielding cheese** and **tangy yogurt** are as easily performed at home, albeit on a smaller scale, without taking away from the **delights** of their **magical and delicious transformation**.

Butter, cream and yogurt

Generations ago, country cooks would make their own butter, clotted cream and yogurt to use up surplus milk supplies that otherwise would have spoiled. Nowadays of course, there is no incentive: supermarkets offer an abundance of these products, and surely it takes up too much time and would need hard-to-learn, long-forgotten domestic skills? The good news is that simple dairy products are easily achievable by the home cook and extremely satisfying to make.

Modern equipment such as free-standing mixers may not be as aesthetically pleasing as an old-fashioned butter churn but it takes away all the hard work, enabling butter to be created in a matter of minutes. Yogurt simply needs to be left in an airing cupboard overnight and clotted cream can be cooked on the kitchen hob. If you need any more encouragement, just imagine your own creamy butter and tangy yogurt served at breakfast or a dollop of clotted cream with scones and jam...

Dairy kitchenalia

There is a wealth of secondhand dairy items available that will make your finished butter look even more appealing. Butter pats, moulds and stamps as well as old-fashioned churns and dairy thermometers can be found on auction websites, in antiques shops and, if you're lucky, at car boot sales. Butter pats are quite common and you can pick up a reasonable pair for very little. Prices of moulds depend on their size and rarity.

Butter

PREPARATION **10 MINUTES**

*Makes about 600g (1lb 3oz) butter
and 600ml (1 pint) buttermilk*
1.2 litres (2 pints) double cream
¼ teaspoon salt (optional)

Making butter is very simple: double cream needs to be shaken or beaten to a point where the buttermilk and butterfat separate. This can be done in an old-fashioned churn, by shaking the cream vigorously in a jam jar (which takes at least 30 minutes) or by the easiest method, a free-standing mixer. If you use the latter, don't make my mistake and leave it unattended. I went out of the pantry to stir some frying onions in the kitchen. I heard a thud (the separation of butter and buttermilk), then a large splash as the buttermilk shot into the air covering the walls, worktop and floor!

1 Remove the cream from the fridge 1–2 hours before you want to make the butter so that it comes to room temperature.

2 Pour the cream into the bowl of a free-standing mixer with the K-beater (the whisk attachment used for heavy beating or whipping) attached. Beat on medium speed. Keep watch as it will suddenly separate into lumps of butter and a pool of buttermilk. Strain off the buttermilk into a jug and chill until needed. You can drink it or use it to make Buttermilk Scones (see page 80) and Wholemeal Soda Bread (see page 18).

3 Put the lumps of butter into a colander and, with the cold tap running, gently squeeze and knead to remove excess buttermilk – gradually the liquid you squeeze out will run clear. You must do this or the butter will go rancid very quickly. Using butter pats will press out the liquid in the same way.

4 To make salted butter, add a scant ¼ teaspoon salt and knead in thoroughly. Taste – if it's too salty, you can rinse it out with cold water again.

5 Wrap in wax or greaseproof paper. Unsalted butter keeps for 2–3 days in the fridge; salted butter for up to 1 week; both can be frozen for up to 1 month.

Anchovy butter

Herb butter

Cinnamon butter

Variations

Cinnamon butter

Mash 125g (4oz) butter with
3 teaspoons ground cinnamon and
3 teaspoons soft brown sugar. Shape
into a log, wrap in wax or greaseproof
paper and chill or freeze. Spread on
toast or crumpets.

Herb butter

Mash 125g (4oz) butter with
2 tablespoons freshly chopped herbs,
such as parsley, mint, tarragon or
chives. Shape into a log, wrap in wax or
greaseproof paper and chill or freeze.
Cut into 1cm (½ inch) discs and melt on
steaks, pork and lamb chops, chicken
and fish.

Anchovy butter

Mash 125g (4oz) butter with 1 tablespoon
freshly chopped parsley, 6 anchovy
fillets, 1 finely chopped shallot and the
juice of half a lemon. Shape into a log,
wrap in wax or greaseproof paper and
chill or freeze. Cut into 1cm (½ inch)
discs and melt on steaks, pork and lamb
chops, chicken and fish.

Buttermilk scones

Use the buttermilk left over from butter-making (see page 78) – if you use commercial buttermilk you will need slightly more than 150ml (¼ pint).

1 Preheat the oven to 220ºC (200ºC fan oven/425°F), gas mark 7.
2 Sift the flour, salt and baking powder into a bowl. Rub in the butter until the mixture resembles breadcrumbs.
3 With a flat-bladed knife, mix in the buttermilk to make a soft, but not too sticky dough.
4 Turn out onto a lightly floured worksurface, knead very lightly and briefly to bring together, then pat into a circle about 2cm (¾ inch) thick. Cut out rounds with a 6cm (2½ inch) cutter and put, spaced apart, onto a lightly greased baking sheet. Brush with beaten egg or milk.
5 Bake in the oven for 12–15 minutes until risen and golden. Cool on a wire rack, then serve with jam and lots of homemade clotted cream (see page 81).

PREPARATION **15 MINUTES**
COOKING **12–15 MINUTES**

Makes 6–8 scones
225g (7½oz) self-raising flour
a pinch of salt
1 teaspoon baking powder
40g (1½oz) cold butter, diced, plus extra
  for greasing
100–150ml (3½fl oz–¼ pint) buttermilk
beaten egg or milk, to glaze

Clotted cream

Traditionally, clotted cream was made from cream that was left to rise to the surface of the milk in the dairy then 'cooked' in large shallow pans until it formed a golden crust. Here, I've made it with a carton of double cream – it's even better made with Jersey cream if you can get it.

PREPARATION **5 MINUTES PLUS COOLING**
COOKING **ABOUT 5 HOURS**

Makes 150–300ml (¼–½ pint)
300–600ml (½–1 pint) double cream, or however much you want to make

1 Put the cream into a double boiler or bain marie set over the lowest heat. If you don't have a double boiler, put the cream into a heatproof bowl set inside a pan. Pour in enough hot water so that it comes halfway up the sides of the bowl. Leave to gently cook for about 5 hours undisturbed until a golden crust forms on the surface. The cream must not bubble or boil.
2 Cover and leave overnight in a cool place, then spoon off the clotted cream and transfer to the fridge until needed. The double cream left underneath can be used as usual in recipes.

Clotted cream fudge

Replace the vanilla extract with a few drops of coffee or almond essence for a change of flavour.

PREPARATION **15 MINUTES PLUS COOLING**
COOKING **30 MINUTES**

Makes about 625g (1 ¼lb)
275g (9oz) caster sugar
110g (3½oz) golden syrup
225g (7½oz) Clotted Cream (see above)
½ teaspoon vanilla extract

1 Put all the ingredients except the vanilla into a heavy-based pan and set over a low heat to dissolve the sugar. Lightly grease a 20cm (8 inch) square tin.
2 Turn up the heat and boil the mixture until it reaches 100°C (212°F) on a sugar thermometer. Turn the heat down to a steady but not raging boil until the temperature reaches 116°C (240°F) – up to 20 minutes. Stir frequently to stop the mixture catching on the base of the pan.
3 Carefully pour the fudge into a bowl, stir in the vanilla and leave to stand until the temperature has dropped to 50°C (122°F). Beat vigorously until the fudge thickens and turns from glossy to matt. Turn into the tin and level with the back of a spoon. Leave to set and cut into squares when completely cold.

Plain yogurt

Save a little of your first batch to make your next. Straining it through a muslin bag gives a Greek-style yogurt. It is also delicious drizzled with runny honey.

PREPARATION **10 MINUTES PLUS SETTING**

Makes about 750ml (1¼ pints)
750ml (1¼ pints) whole milk
2 tablespoons full-fat plain yogurt

1 Bring the milk to the boil in a pan set over a medium heat. Take off the heat and leave to cool to about 43°C (109°F). Put the yogurt in a large ceramic or earthenware bowl.
2 When the milk has cooled to the correct temperature, remove the skin and whisk into the yogurt.
3 Put the ceramic bowl into another larger bowl and pour boiling water in between. Wrap the bowls in a large towel, covering the yogurt completely, and leave in a warm place, ideally an airing cupboard, for at least 4 hours. The yogurt should set firm. If not, check again after an hour – the longer you leave it the thicker and sharper tasting it will be. Store in the fridge until needed for up to 1 week.

Cucumber yogurt dip

Serve this fresh, tangy dip with strips of toasted wholemeal pitta bread or as an accompaniment to a spicy curry.

PREPARATION **15 MINUTES**

Makes about 250g (8oz)
half a cucumber, deseeded and diced
a pinch of ground cumin
1 tablespoon freshly chopped coriander
1 tablespoon freshly chopped mint, plus extra to garnish
200ml (7fl oz) homemade Plain Yogurt (see opposite)

1 Mix together all of the ingredients, reserving a spoonful of the cucumber, and season with sea salt to taste. Serve in a small dish topped with the reserved cucumber and some chopped mint.

Scented yogurt cooler

Traditionally this type of drink tends to be rather sweet, so start off with half the amount of sugar, then tweak and add to suit your palate.

PREPARATION **10 MINUTES**

Makes about 400ml (14fl oz) or 2 glasses
350ml (12fl oz) homemade Plain Yogurt (see opposite)
1 tablespoon orange flower water or rose water
3 tablespoons double cream
3–6 tablespoons caster sugar
a handful of ice cubes

1 Put all of the ingredients into a blender or food processor and blitz until combined. Pour into tall glasses and serve the drink immediately.

Soft cheeses

Country kitchens of old would turn their surplus milk supplies into pillowy mounds of fresh, mild cheese. The modern cook has no such need, yet it's a skill that's easy to master and brings much pleasure. Within hours and with little effort, cow's or goat's milk can be transformed into a refreshing soft cheese to be enjoyed on crusty bread, in a salad or turned into a tangy cheesecake.

My grandmother made cheese with soured milk and a piece of muslin. She'd hang the bundle by the back door, until the whey dripped away and a soft cheese could be unwrapped. You will also need rennet, a chemical found in calves' stomachs that will curdle milk and separate the curds, and whey for cheese making. Vegetarian rennet is available from good health food shops. Alternatively, lemon juice or vinegar will do a similar job.

Fresh ricotta

This versatile fresh cheese can be used in a variety of sweet or savoury recipes.

PREPARATION **10 MINUTES PLUS STANDING**
COOKING **5 MINUTES**

Makes about 500g (1lb)
**1.8 litres (3 pints) unhomogenized
  whole milk**
**3 tablespoons distilled white vinegar
  or 4 tablespoons lemon juice or a
  few drops of rennet**
salt

1 Put the milk into a stainless steel saucepan and stir in the vinegar, lemon juice or rennet.
2 Put the pan over a very low heat and bring the milk up to a temperature of 95°C (203°F).
3 Remove from the heat and leave undisturbed in a warm place – between 25°C–40°C (77–104°F) for about 6 hours or until it separates into solid curds and liquid whey.

4 Line a sieve with muslin and ladle in the curds and whey. Once drained you should be left with ricotta that has the consistency of thick yogurt. For a firmer ricotta, draw the muslin into a bag and hang up over a bowl in a cool place to drain until the desired texture is reached.
5 Add salt to taste and store in the fridge for up to 5 days. It is at its best eaten after 24 hours.

Baked ricotta cheesecake

For a change, use ginger biscuits for the base and replace the lemon with the zest of a large orange or a couple of limes.

PREPARATION **25 MINUTES PLUS CHILLING**
COOKING **45 MINUTES**

Serves 6–8

175g (6oz) oat biscuits, crushed
50g (2oz) butter, melted
225g (7½oz) homemade Ricotta (see opposite), drained
3 large eggs
125g (4oz) caster sugar
175g (6oz) full-fat plain yogurt
finely grated zest of 2 large lemons
50g (2oz) sultanas

1 Preheat the oven to 160°C (140°C fan oven/325°F), gas mark 3.
2 Mix together the biscuits and butter and press into the base of a deep 20cm (8 inch) cake tin. Chill for 30 minutes.
3 Beat together the remaining ingredients, except the sultanas, until smooth. Stir in the sultanas.

Pour into the cake tin and bake in the oven for 45 minutes until lightly golden and just set.
4 Turn off the oven and leave the cheesecake inside to cool with the oven door ajar – this should stop the surface cracking. Chill until ready to serve and consume within 3 days.

Soft goat's cheese

Don't throw away the whey as you can use it to replace water in breadmaking. Warm it gently until tepid before using. It freezes well until you need it, too.

PREPARATION **10 MINUTES PLUS SETTING**

Makes about 1kg (2lb)
2 litres (3½ pints) whole goat's milk
8 drops rennet, mixed with cooled boiled water
finely chopped herbs (optional)
salt (optional)

1 Heat the milk to 80°C (176°F), then stir in the rennet. Leave to cool for a few hours until the milk is set.
2 Line a colander with sterilized muslin. Cut the curd into cubes and gently spoon into the muslin. Gather in the corners, tie with string and hang over a bowl in a cool place for the whey to drain away. The longer you leave it to hang the firmer it will become. For soft cheese, leave for about 3 hours; for firm cheese about 6 hours.
3 Shape the cheese as you wish. For example, roll into a log shape, then roll in finely chopped herbs. Salting the cheese means it will keep for up to 1 week.

Tip
You can also use the same method to make a basic soft cheese with whole cow's milk.

Goat's cheese toasts

Serve these toasts as a starter for six or a light lunch for two.

PREPARATION **5 MINUTES**
COOKING **ABOUT 10 MINUTES**

Serves 6
6 slices French bread
1–2 tablespoons walnut oil
1 garlic clove, sliced in half lengthways
125g (4oz) homemade Soft Goat's Cheese formed into a log
  and cut into 2.5cm (1 inch) slices
salad leaves, to serve

1 Preheat the oven to 180°C (160°C fan oven/350°F), gas mark 4. Brush the bread on both sides with the oil and rub with the cut side of the garlic clove.
2 Arrange the bread on a baking sheet and bake in the oven for 5 minutes. Put a slice of cheese on top of each piece of bread and return to the oven for 5–7 minutes until the cheese is soft but not melted. Serve with salad leaves.

A simple goat's cheese salad

Try rolling the homemade goat's cheese in dried chilli flakes or crushed black or mixed peppercorns.

PREPARATION **15 MINUTES**
COOKING **10 MINUTES**

Serves 4

2 thick slices fresh country-style bread

1 tablespoon rapeseed oil

200g (7oz) homemade Soft Goat's Cheese (see page 88)

2 tablespoons freshly chopped mixed herbs (such as parsley, chives and lemon thyme)

3 tablespoons hazelnut oil

1 tablespoon white wine vinegar

1 garlic clove, crushed

a squeeze of lemon juice

200g (7oz) salad leaves

40g (1½oz) roughly chopped and toasted hazelnuts

salt and freshly ground black pepper

croutons, to serve

1 Preheat the oven to 200°C (180°C fan oven/400°F), gas mark 6.

2 Cut the fresh country-style bread into cubes and toss in the rapeseed oil. Spread out onto a baking sheet. Bake in the oven for 10 minutes until golden and crispy. Set aside to cool.

3 Shape the soft goat's cheese into a log, then roll in the freshly chopped mixed herbs. Chill until firm.

4 Put the hazelnut oil and white wine vinegar into a screw-top jar with the crushed garlic, lemon juice and plenty of seasoning. Shake well to combine.

5 Just before serving, gently toss the salad leaves with the dressing. Divide between 4 plates, top with slices of goat's cheese and garnish with the toasted hazelnuts and croutons. Add a final flourish of freshly ground pepper.

Mascarpone

You can find tartaric acid in good chemists or from home-brewing websites.

PREPARATION **5 MINUTES PLUS CHILLING**
COOKING **ABOUT 10 MINUTES**

Makes about 400g (13oz)
600ml (1 pint) double cream
a large pinch of tartaric acid
icing sugar (optional)

1 Put the cream into a stainless steel pan and heat gently to 80°C (176°F). Add the tartaric acid and stir constantly for 10 minutes. Curds should form.
2 Line a colander with muslin and spoon in the curds and whey. Leave to allow the whey to drain away thoroughly.
3 Put the colander in a bowl in the fridge and leave to drain overnight. Sweeten with icing sugar if you like.

Mascarpone sauce for pasta

Choose a pasta such as spaghetti or linguine so that the creamy sauce clings to the strands.

PREPARATION **5 MINUTES**
COOKING **ABOUT 10 MINUTES**

Serves 2
150–200g (5–7oz) pasta
3 tablespoons homemade Mascarpone (see previous recipe)
2 egg yolks
50g (2oz) grated Parmesan, plus extra to serve
a drizzle of olive oil
100g (3½oz) prosciutto or streaky bacon, chopped
a few chopped sage leaves
freshly ground black pepper

1 Cook the pasta according to the packet instructions.
2 Meanwhile, mix together the mascarpone, yolks and Parmesan. Heat the oil in a small pan and fry the prosciutto or bacon until golden.
3 Drain the pasta, reserving a few tablespoons of the cooking water. Return the pasta to the pan and toss with the mascarpone mixture and prosciutto or bacon. Stir in enough of the pasta water to make a creamy sauce.
4 Serve at once with the sage, plenty of Parmesan and plenty of black pepper.

Fresh mascarpone with berries

Fresh mascarpone has a tangy yet creamy flavour that works especially well with soft summer berries in place of whipped double cream.

PREPARATION **15 MINUTES PLUS MACERATING**

Serves 6

400g (13oz) mixed soft summer berries

4–5 tablespoons sweet dessert wine (such as Muscat de Beaumes de Venise)

1 tablespoon icing sugar

250g (8oz) homemade Mascarpone (see page 90)

250ml (8fl oz) whipping cream

a few drops vanilla extract

1 Put the mixed berries into a bowl with 2–3 tablespoons of the sweet dessert wine and leave to macerate for 1 hour for the fruit to release its juices.

2 Beat the remaining sweet dessert wine and the icing sugar with the mascarpone until smooth.

3 In a separate bowl, whip the whipping cream to soft peaks with the vanilla extract. Gently fold into the mascarpone mixture.

4 Layer the mascarpone mixture and fruit in 6 serving glasses, finishing with a layer of fruit.

Ice cream and sorbets

Creamy or refreshing, rich or zesty, ice creams, sorbets and granitas add a welcome touch of luxury to the country cook's practical repertoire. Once a sign of wealth and privilege by those who could afford ice houses at sumptuous Victorian feasts, the advent of home freezers now makes the art accessible to all and no less irresistible. You will be rewarded with a deliciousness that belies the simplicity of the ingredients: the creamiest milk and freshest eggs combined with a touch of sugar and the freshest, ripest berries or darkest chocolate is all that's required for pure bliss.

INGREDIENTS

Ice creams and sorbets are at their best when made from good-quality, simple ingredients. **Fruit** should be fresh and perfectly ripe, especially when making sorbets as they will only be mixed with sugar syrup, so the flavour needs to shine through. Acid fruits, such as **citrus**, **berries** and **passion fruit** make particularly good sorbets. However, certain fruits like **pineapple** and **kiwi fruit** contain an enzyme called bromelain that hinders or prevents successful freezing. Use **alcohol** sparingly – too much will also inhibit the freezing process and can make an ice cream taste harsh. White granulated and caster **sugars** are preferable for crystal clear sugar syrups to add sweetness and hinder the formation of too many ice crystals; too much sugar though and the ice will remain slushy. Higher fat content **milk** and **cream** give a richer, smoother taste and also prevent too many ice crystals forming; however, too much in proportion to other ingredients will make it dense and crumbly. **Crème fraîche** adds a pleasant sour note while **yogurt** retains its characteristic flavour and is lower in fat. A squeeze of **lemon juice** balances sweetness while a pinch of **salt** heightens flavours. **Nuts** and **chocolate chips** add pleasing texture and crunch and should be added when the ice cream has been churned. Adding **rosemary**, **mint** or **basil** to sorbets creates elegant palate cleansers.

EQUIPMENT

Electric **ice-cream makers** are desirable but not essential: excellent ice cream can be made with a hand **whisk**, a bit of elbow grease and frequent attention (the still-freezing method). However, when making smooth sorbets and custard-based ice creams their constant churning does prevent ice crystals from forming in the mixture. The most expensive ice-cream makers have a built in refrigeration unit that chills the mixture while it churns; cheaper models have removable containers that need to be put in the freezer for 24 hours before churning. The drawback with the latter is that they need to be frozen again before you can make more, whereas another batch of ice cream can be made immediately with the more sophisticated versions. Granitas are the simplest ices to make: their coarse, granular texture is achieved by frequent stirring with a fork every 30 minutes during the freezing process to break up ice crystals. When making mousse and meringue-

based parfaits, an **electric hand-beater** for whisking cream, a **sugar thermometer** and a **heavy-based saucepan** for making sugar syrups are also useful. Metal ice-cream **moulds** can be used to create intricately shaped parfaits – look for them at antique fairs and scour junk shops. Otherwise, a **loaf tin** lined with **cling film** is an adequate substitute.

A BIT OF TECHNIQUE

• If you don't have an ice-cream maker, you will need to use the still-freezing method. Put the mixture in a shallow freezerproof container and freeze for 2 hours or until ice crystals form at the edges. Turn into a bowl and beat with an electric hand-beater. Pour back into the container and return to the freezer. Repeat every 2 hours until the ice cream or sorbet is completely frozen.
• It is possible to add extra smoothness to sorbets: when almost fully frozen, blitz quickly with one egg white in a blender or food processor, then return to the freezer until solid.
• Before churning or still-freezing, fruit purées, sugar syrups and custard bases should be completely cold.
• Always scald (bring to just below boiling point) milk before using in ice-cream bases – it will give a smoother mouthfeel to the finished ice cream.
• Custard bases benefit from standing in the fridge for up to 24 hours to develop their flavours.
• When making parfaits, never fill the mould to the top to allow room for expansion as it freezes; to unmould dip the mould very briefly into hot water.
• Remember that the ice cream or sorbet mixture should be overly sweet or strong tasting because freezing mutes flavour.
• Removing from the freezer 30 minutes before serving will improve taste and texture.
• Do not refreeze ice cream once it has melted as it can contain potentially harmful bacteria that could cause food poisoning.

Top left: scalded milk is infused with a vanilla pod;
Top right: blending the freshest egg yolks with caster sugar;
Bottom left: gently cooking the custard base until thickened; draw your finger across the wooden spoon to test if it is the right consistency;
Bottom right: whisking the partially frozen ice cream every 2 hours if making by hand.

Rich vanilla ice cream

This ice cream is made with a custard base, which can be adapted and flavoured with fruit purées, chocolate or coffee. It keeps for up to 1 month in the freezer.

PREPARATION **40 MINUTES PLUS FREEZING**
COOKING **5 MINUTES**

Serves 4–6
1 vanilla pod
300ml (½ pint) whole milk
4 egg yolks
125g (4oz) caster sugar
300ml (½ pint) whipping or double cream

1 Split the vanilla pod lengthways and scrape out the seeds. Put the pod and seeds in a saucepan with the milk over medium heat. Heat the milk until hot but not boiling, then take off the heat and leave to infuse for 30 minutes.
2 Mix together the egg yolks and sugar in a medium bowl. Remove and discard the vanilla pod and blend the milk into the yolk mixture using a wooden spoon or a whisk.
3 Rinse the milk saucepan and return the milk and egg mixture to the dry saucepan. Cook over a low to medium heat, stirring constantly until the mixture has thickened enough to coat the back of a wooden spoon. Be careful not to overheat or the mixture will curdle.
4 Pass the mixture through a sieve into a chilled bowl. Transfer the bowl to the fridge to chill – this is your custard base (which you can go on to add other flavours to if you wish).
5 Stir in the cream, then churn in an electric ice-cream maker following the manufacturer's instructions or transfer to a shallow freezerproof container, put in the freezer and beat every 2 hours until the texture is creamy (see page 94).

Lavender and honey ice cream

To make lavender sugar, bury the flowers from 2 sprigs of fresh or dried lavender into a large jar of caster sugar. Leave to infuse for 2 weeks before using.

PREPARATION **40 MINUTES PLUS FREEZING**
COOKING **5 MINUTES**

Serves 4–6
1 quantity Rich Vanilla ice Cream custard base (see previous recipe), made with 125g (4oz) lavender sugar (see above)
2 tablespoons lavender honey
300ml (½ pint) whipping or double cream

1 Make the rich vanilla custard base as described in the previous recipe, replacing the caster sugar with lavender sugar. If you cannot find lavender sugar, infuse the milk with 12 heads of lightly bruised lavender.
2 Stir in the honey and cream, then chill until cold. Churn in an electric ice-cream maker following the manufacturer's instructions or transfer to a shallow freezerproof container, put in the freezer and beat every 2 hours until the texture is creamy (see page 94).

Nutmeg and bay leaf ice cream

This subtle and delicate ice cream is particularly delicious served with warm apple pie.

PREPARATION **40 MINUTES PLUS FREEZING**
COOKING **5 MINUTES**

Serves 4–6
1 quantity Rich Vanilla ice Cream custard base (see recipe on this page), made with 3 large bay leaves
1 teaspoon grated nutmeg
300ml (½ pint) whipping or double cream

1 Make the rich vanilla custard base as described in the previous recipe, infusing the milk in step 1 with the bay leaves instead of the vanilla pod.
2 Stir in the nutmeg and cream and then chill until cold. Churn in an electric ice-cream maker following the manufacturer's instructions or transfer to a shallow freezerproof container, put in the freezer and beat every 2 hours until the texture is creamy (see page 94).

Nutmeg and bay leaf ice cream

Lavender and honey ice cream

Rich vanilla ice cream

Blackcurrant and mint ice cream

Meringue-based ice creams don't need to be churned and work particularly well with tart-tasting fruits that balance the sweetness of the base mixture.

PREPARATION **30 MINUTES PLUS FREEZING**
COOKING **10 MINUTES**

Serves 4–6
a small handful of mint leaves
300g (10oz) blackcurrants
250ml (8fl oz) water
2 tablespoons crème de cassis
250g (9oz) caster sugar
2 egg whites
**300ml (½ pint) whipping or
    double cream**
a squeeze of lemon juice

1 Roughly bruise the mint leaves in a pestle and mortar to release their oils and put in a saucepan with the blackcurrants and 100ml (3½fl oz) of the water. Heat gently until the berries soften and release their juices, about 5 minutes.

2 Push the blackcurrants and mint through a sieve into a bowl. Add the cassis and leave to cool.

3 Dampen 4–6 individual moulds with water and line with cling film that overlaps the edges. Alternatively, you can use a 1kg (1¾lb) loaf tin.

4 Dissolve the sugar in a saucepan with the remaining water over a gentle heat. Bring to the boil, then simmer, without stirring, until it reaches 120°C (250°F) – firm-ball stage (drop a teaspoon of syrup into a bowl of cold water. It should make a firm ball when brought together with your fingers) on a sugar thermometer.

5 Meanwhile, whisk the egg whites in a clean, dry bowl until they make stiff peaks. In a separate bowl, whisk the cream until it just softly peaks.

6 Whisk the hot sugar syrup into the egg whites and continue whisking until the mixture is cooled.

7 Fold the blackcurrant purée into the meringue base along with a squeeze of lemon juice. Then fold in the whipped cream. Turn the mixture into the prepared moulds or loaf tin. Smooth over the surface, fold the excess cling film over the top and freeze for 24 hours.

8 When ready to serve, turn out of the moulds and remove the cling film.

Raspberry ripple parfait

A mousse-based ice cream doesn't need to be churned and the flavours can be varied with other fruit purées. As an alternative to ripples, you can completely combine the mousse base and cream with the purée for a more amalgamated mixture. This parfait will keep in the freezer for up to 3 months.

PREPARATION **30 MINUTES PLUS FREEZING**
COOKING **5 MINUTES**

Serves 4–6
500g (1lb) raspberries
100g (3½oz) icing sugar, sifted
a squeeze of lemon juice
3 egg yolks
75g (3oz) caster sugar
150ml (¼ pint) water
300ml (½ pint) whipping cream
1 teaspoon vanilla bean paste

1 Line a dampened 1kg (1¾lb) loaf tin with cling film that overlaps the edges.

2 Purée the raspberries in a blender or food processor, then push through a sieve to remove the seeds. Stir in the icing sugar and lemon juice.

3 Put the egg yolks in a heatproof bowl and whisk by hand until well beaten, or with electric hand-beaters.

4 Put the granulated sugar in a saucepan with the water and dissolve over a low heat. Bring to the boil, then simmer, without stirring, until it reaches 120°C (250°F) – firm-ball stage (drop a teaspoon of syrup into a bowl of cold water. It should make a firm ball when brought together with your fingers) on a sugar thermometer.

5 Continue whisking the eggs while pouring on the hot sugar syrup in a steady stream. Continue whisking until the mixture is thick, mousse-like and forms a ribbon trail. Leave to cool.

6 Whisk the cream in a separate bowl with the vanilla bean paste until it just holds its shape – it should be about the same consistency as the egg mixture.

7 Fold the cream into the egg mixture. Swirl in the raspberry purée to make ripples, then carefully pour into the prepared loaf tin. Smooth over the surface, fold the excess cling film over the top and freeze for 24 hours.

8 When ready to serve, turn the parfait out of the tin, remove the cling film and cut into slices.

Coffee granita

Eat the granita as soon it's ready – leave it too long in the
freezer and the ice crystals will be hard and crunchy.

PREPARATION 35 MINUTES PLUS FREEZING

Serves 4–6
150g (5oz) soft light brown sugar
300ml (½ pint) hot strong coffee
150ml (¼ pint) coffee liqueur

1 Stir the sugar into the hot strong coffee and mix until
dissolved. Leave to cool.
2 Stir in the liqueur. Pour into a shallow freezerproof container
– the depth of the liquid should be no more than 2.5cm (1 inch)
so divide between a few containers if necessary.
3 Freeze for 30 minutes, then remove from the freezer and
scrape any frozen mixture into the centre with a fork. Return
to the freezer.
4 Repeat every 30 minutes until completely frozen with a
grainy texture. Serve immediately.

Mango and passion fruit yogurt ice

Using a full-fat yogurt produces a richer, smoother result; lower-fat versions produce a grainier texture.

PREPARATION **20 MINUTES PLUS FREEZING**
COOKING **2 MINUTES**

Serves 4–6
1 small ripe mango, peeled, stoned and chopped
juice of 1 lemon
150g (5oz) caster sugar
2 medium eggs
4 passion fruit
1 x 500g (1lb) tub Greek yogurt

1 Purée the chopped mango in a blender or food processor until smooth.
2 Put the puréed mango, lemon juice, sugar, eggs and passion fruit in a saucepan and cook for 2 minutes until thickened. Push through a sieve into a bowl to remove any fibrous strands and seeds. Cover the surface with cling film to stop a skin forming and chill until it's cold.
3 Fold the Greek yogurt into the fruit mixture. For a smoother result, churn in an electric ice-cream maker following the manufacturer's instructions, or transfer to a shallow freezerproof container and freeze without mixing if preferred.

Mint sorbet

Sorbets should be eaten within 2–3 days.

PREPARATION **15 MINUTES PLUS FREEZING**
COOKING **ABOUT 10 MINUTES**

Serves 4–6
450g (14½oz) granulated sugar
700ml (24fl oz) water
a large handful of mint leaves
grated zest and juice of 1 lime

1 Dissolve the sugar in a saucepan with the water over a gentle heat. Bruise the mint leaves in a pestle and mortar and add to the saucepan along with the lime zest. Bring to the boil, then simmer for 5 minutes. Take off the heat and leave to infuse for 30 minutes. Add the lime juice and strain into a bowl. Chill until cold.
2 Churn in an electric ice-cream maker following the manufacturer's instructions or transfer to a shallow freezerproof container, put in the freezer and beat every 2 hours until the texture is smooth.

Preserving

For country cooks, turning a glut of fruit or vegetables into a stock of preserves to fill the pantry or larder is immensely satisfying. They're surprisingly cheap to make too, especially if you take time to do a little hedgerow foraging for extra seasonal ingredients. Late summer and autumn are the traditional time for picking and preserving the garden's bumper crops of fruit and vegetables but there is nearly always some suitable product to make the basis of a chutney, jam, jelly or marmalade whatever the time of year.

Marmalade

Can days begin any better than with smells of toast and coffee curling up the stairs and a jar of homemade marmalade catching the morning sunlight? The word marmalade has evolved from the middle ages originating from the Portuguese word *marmelada,* which was their name for quince paste (a bit like the Membrillo paste that's served with manchego cheese today).

Marmalade originally had a paste-like consistency and was made from all types of fruit.

Eventually more sugar and the peel of citrus fruits were added during the 18th century to make the consistency we know today. Bitter oranges like the Seville orange were preferred for their flavour. Generally, marmalade differs from jam in that it tends to have a bitter flavour rather than sweet.

Marmalade was first fashionable as a part of the dessert course at banquets, and migrated to the breakfast table by way of the medicine chest and a reputation for curing rheums and colds.

From left to right:
Thick-cut Seville orange marmalade;
Three fruit marmalade (at back);
Clementine marmalade (at front);
and Lemon and honey marmalade.

INGREDIENTS

New Year is the traditional time for marmalade making as it marks the short season of **Seville oranges**, which appear for a few weeks only in late January and February. Sevilles are spared the anti-fungal wax treatment given to other citrus fruits, so won't need such a ruthless scrubbing. But don't let tradition hold you back. As we have mentioned, all sorts of citrus varieties make lovely marmalade. **Grapefruit** and **lemons** share a tantalizing bitterness with Sevilles, while sweet oranges and all the loose-skinned varieties such as **clementines**, **tangerines** and **satsumas** have their own distinctive flavours. Sevilles, grapefruit and lemons have lots of **pectin** and **acid**, the two ingredients that, when combined with sugar, ensure a well-set preserve. Sugar is the other essential ingredient and there is a wide choice. The cheapest is white **granulated sugar**. **Preserving sugar** has larger, easily dissolved crystals and makes beautifully clear gels. **Less refined sugars** make good-looking marmalades if they are pale. **Dark, unrefined sugars** are useful for adding colour and flavour but will be only a small proportion of the total amount used in any recipe. **Jam sugar** has added pectin for a sure-fire set.

EQUIPMENT

The kit required is fairly straightforward. A **preserving pan**, wider at the rim than the base, is ideal because it encourages rapid evaporation and is large enough to allow the fast-boiling preserve to rise without boiling over. A sizeable **casserole** or **large pan** is a better substitute than a tall pasta boiler or stock pot. Add a clean **board**, a very **sharp knife**, a **lemon squeezer** or reamer, a **sieve**, some **butter muslin** and **string**, **recycled jars**, **lids** or **jam pot covers**, a **wooden spoon**, a couple of **bowls** and a **ladle** and you are nearly there. The only specialist piece of kit I would not be without is a cheap-as-chips **jam funnel**, which allows you to fill the hot jars with a minimum of sticky drips and dribbles.

MAKING CHIP MARMALADE

I like what is called chip marmalade, which has pieces of tender peel suspended in a richly flavoured gel. This is what we'll be making. The second type, equally traditional, pulverizes whole cooked fruit and makes dense, opaque marmalade that is quick and simple to produce, but not quite so good to eat or look at.

The essential thing with chip marmalade is to cook the chopped peel until it is really tender – tender enough to squish between finger and thumb – before adding the sugar. When the sugar goes in, stir the mixure over a low heat until every grain has melted before turning up the heat and boiling to setting point. Take your time. Leave an undissolved grain or two of sugar and your marmalade may crystallize in its pot as the sugar reverts.

JUDGING SETTING POINT

This requires attention and a little skill. Don't hurry. Prepare a stack of small plates or saucers by chilling them in the fridge. Bring the marmalade mixture to a rolling boil that cannot be stirred down. Let it boil for about 10 minutes, then start testing for a set. Take the pan off the heat and drop a teaspoonful of the marmalade on a chilled saucer. Leave it for a minute and then push it with your finger. When the mixture thickens enough to wrinkle, it will set. If it stays runny, return the pan to the boil for a few more minutes, then test again. It should not need more than 20 minutes altogether. The variability depends on the fruit and how much evaporation has taken place while tenderizing the chips.

POTTING YOUR MARMALADE

When setting point is reached, take the pan off the heat, skim off any froth and allow the marmalade to cool and thicken enough to hold its peel in suspension. Now ladle it into the warm, sterilized jars. If you are using wax paper discs and transparent jam pot covers, put on the wax discs now, cover the batch with a clean cloth and leave until completely cold before applying the covers. If you are using lids, cover with a clean cloth until completely cold before putting on the lids. Covering warm jars results in condensation, which encourages mould to form. If you are making different types of marmalade, label while you still remember which is which.

STERILIZING

To sterilize jars, lids, seals and funnels, wash in hot, soapy water and put in the oven preheated to 150°C (130°C fan oven/300°F) gas mark 2 for 20 minutes.

Top left: boil vigorously to bring the marmalade to setting point;
Top right: leave the marmalade to stand before potting;
Bottom left: testing for setting point;
Bottom right: pot the marmalade while it is still hot.

Thick-cut Seville orange marmalade

Adding a slug of whisky or cider brandy just before potting the marmalade adds flavour. Don't worry about consuming spirits at breakfast time – the heat of the marmalade evaporates the alcohol, leaving only extra flavour.

PREPARATION **40 MINUTES PLUS SOAKING**
COOKING **2½ HOURS**

Makes about 2kg (4lb)
1kg (2lb) Seville oranges
1 lemon
2 litres (3½ pints) water
2kg (4lb) preserving sugar
200g (7oz) dark muscovado sugar
75ml (3fl oz) whisky or cider brandy

1 Wash and dry the fruit, and cut in halves or quarters.
2 Set a sieve over a bowl and line it with a large double layer of muslin.
3 Working over the sieve, juice the fruit, scouring the shells as you go, and dropping the pips, squeezed flesh and membranes into the cloth. A reamer is usually the easiest way to empty oranges and lemons cleanly. Reserve the juice squeezed from the fruit.
4 Tie all the residue into a loose bag and put it in a preserving pan with the water.
5 Shred the skins as finely as you like and add to the pan. Leave to soak for several hours or, better still, overnight.
6 Bring to the boil, reduce the heat and simmer uncovered until the peel is meltingly tender and the liquid has reduced by half – usually about 2 hours, but sometimes more. Cover the pan if too much evaporation is occurring before the peel is tender.
7 Remove the bag of pips and bits and squeeze the liquid out of it back into the pan. Discard the contents of the bag. Add the sugar to the pan, plus the reserved juice.
8 Bring slowly to the boil, stirring until the sugar has dissolved completely. Raise the heat and boil hard until setting point (see page 106) is reached, usually about 10 minutes. Leave to cool and thicken a little, then stir to re-distribute the peel. Add the whisky and stir in before potting.

Variations

Lemon and honey marmalade

The inspiration for this marmalade is everyone's favourite cold cure. Choose a strongly flavoured honey – you are using only a small amount in relation to the quantity of fruit – and cut the peel in short, stubby lengths.

PREPARATION **40 MINUTES PLUS SOAKING**
COOKING **2½ HOURS**

Makes about 2.5kg (5lb)
1kg (2lb) unwaxed lemons
3 litres (5 pints) water
2kg (4lb) preserving sugar
300ml (½ pint) well-perfumed runny honey

1 Follow the recipe above for Thick-cut Seville orange marmalade. Add the honey to the pan in step 7 with the sugar and reserved juices.

Three fruit marmalade

Choose citrus fruit that are heavy for their size to ensure maximum juiciness.

PREPARATION **40 MINUTES PLUS SOAKING**
COOKING **2½ HOURS**

Makes about 1.5kg (3lb)
1 grapefruit
2 oranges
2 lemons
2 litres (3½ pints) water
2kg (4lb) preserving sugar

1 Follow the recipe above for Thick-cut Seville orange marmalade. In step 3, in the case of grapefruit it is easier to quarter them, use a teaspoon inserted between the skin and the flesh to pick up a strip of membrane large enough to grip, then use your fingers to tear out the interior of the fruit, leaving a tidy shell (instead of using a reamer).

Pink grapefruit marmalade

Thick-cut Seville orange marmalade

Clementine marmalade (see page 110)

Lemon and honey marmalade

Pink grapefruit marmalade

Grapefruit has a distinctive bitter edge very similar to Seville oranges, which makes it the best substitute for Sevilles when they are out of season.

PREPARATION **40 MINUTES PLUS SOAKING**
COOKING **2½ HOURS**

Makes about 2.5kg (5lb)
1kg (2lb) pink grapefruit, about 4 medium size
3 litres (5 pints) water
2.25kg (4½lb) granulated or preserving sugar
125ml (4fl oz) freshly squeezed lemon juice

1 Follow the recipe opposite for Thick-cut Seville orange marmalade. In step 3, in the case of grapefruit it is easier to quarter them, use a teaspoon inserted between the skin and the flesh to pick up a strip of membrane large enough to grip, then use your fingers to tear out the interior of the fruit, leaving a tidy shell (instead of using a reamer). Also, in step 7, add the lemon juice at the same time as the sugar and reserved juice.

Clementine marmalade

Tangerines, mandarins and other similar loose-skinned citrus in season can be substituted for clementines. The generous quantity of lemon juice in this recipe helps to overcome the lack of pectin in these sweet citrus varieties. An alternative is to use jam sugar. Finely sliced peel suits this recipe.

PREPARATION **40 MINUTES PLUS SOAKING**
COOKING **2½ HOURS**

Makes about 1kg (2lb)
500g (1lb) clementines
500ml (17fl oz) apple juice
500ml (17fl oz) water
750g (1½lb) preserving sugar
6 tablespoons freshly squeezed lemon juice

1 Wash and dry the fruit, and cut in halves or quarters.
2 Set a sieve over a bowl and line it with a large double layer of muslin.
3 Working over the sieve, juice the fruit, scouring the shells as you go, and dropping the pips, squeezed flesh and membranes into the cloth. In the case of loose skinned citrus such as clementines it is easier to quarter them, use a teaspoon inserted between the skin and the flesh to pick up a strip of membrane large enough to grip, then use your fingers to tear out the interior of the fruit, leaving a tidy shell.
4 Reserve the juice squeezed from the fruit.
5 Tie all the residue into a loose bag and put it in a preserving pan with the apple juice and water.
6 Shred the skins as finely as you like and add the peel to the pan. Leave to soak for several hours or, better still, overnight.
7 Bring to the boil, reduce the heat and simmer uncovered until the peel is meltingly tender and the liquid has reduced by half – usually about 2 hours, but sometimes more. Cover the pan if too much evaporation is occurring before the peel is tender.
8 Remove the bag of pips and bits and squeeze the liquid out of it back into the pan. Discard the contents of the bag. Add the sugar to the pan, plus the reserved juice and lemon juice.
9 Bring slowly to the boil, stirring until the sugar has dissolved completely. Raise the heat and boil hard until setting point (see page 106) is reached, usually about 10 minutes. Leave to cool and thicken a little, then stir to redistribute the peel before potting.

Marmalade muffins

Clementine marmalade makes a particularly good filling for these springy muffins, but any citrus flavour works well.

PREPARATION **30 MINUTES**
COOKING **20–25 MINUTES**

Makes about 12
225g (7½oz) caster sugar
100g (3½oz) unsalted butter
2 medium eggs
1 teaspoon bicarbonate of soda
225ml (7½fl oz) buttermilk (see page 78)
180g (6oz) plain flour
½ teaspoon salt
finely grated zest of 1 orange
4 tablespoons marmalade

1 Preheat the oven to 200°C (180°C fan oven/400°F), gas mark 6, and line a 12-hole muffin tin with paper cases.
2 Cream the sugar and butter until light and fluffy. Beat in the eggs, one at a time.
3 Stir the bicarbonate of soda into the buttermilk.
4 Sift together the flour and salt and fold into the creamed butter mixture with alternative spoonfuls of the buttermilk. Finally stir in the orange zest.
5 Divide half the mixture between the 12 muffin cases. Put a teaspoonful of marmalade in the centre of each one and top with the remaining mixture.
6 Bake in the oven for 20–25 minutes until well risen and springy to touch. The jammy centres will be very hot, so let the muffins cool a little before tasting them.

Jams and jellies

For country cooks, it is a satisfying time of year when the gluts of summer and autumn can be turned into delicious jams and jellies. Wild sloes, blackberries and crab apples are all suitable for preserving while garden orchards are laden with a surplus of plums, pears and quinces. If you don't have any fruit trees, visit a pick-your-own farm – it's far cheaper than the supermarket and supports local farmers. Then retreat to the kitchen, switch on the radio and spend a rewarding afternoon chopping, simmering and potting up the fruits of your pickings. The result will be a pleasing stock of jewel-like preserves to cheer up the breakfast table and give your home-baked cakes a makeover.

INGREDIENTS

There's little you need in the way of specific ingredients to create jams and jellies. **Granulated sugar** is sufficient to produce a good set for most fruit but if you are a nervous novice, use **jam sugar** for a belt-and-braces approach – it contains added pectin to ensure success. **Preserving sugar** has larger crystals that will make jellies clearer and sparkling.

Choose firm, slightly under-ripe, unblemished **fruits** – over-ripe fruit contains less pectin. Fruit high in pectin, such as **apples, plums, damsons** and **gooseberries**, will need little help with setting. **Blueberries, apricots, greengages** and **raspberries** contain medium levels, while **strawberries, cherries, peaches** and **rhubarb** contain the lowest amounts.

Adding **lemon juice** will boost pectin levels. **Liquid pectin** is also available in large supermarkets. To make your own liquid pectin, put 4.5kg (9lb) roughly chopped cooking apples (cores, peel, seeds and all) in a large pan with enough water to just cover. Bring to the boil, then simmer for 20 minutes. Pour into a jelly bag and leave to drip overnight. Pour the liquid into a clean pan and boil until reduced by half. Freeze in batches: 150ml (¼ pint) will set about 1kg (2lb) low-pectin fruit.

Stronger-flavoured **redcurrants, blackcurrants, quince, blackberries, sloes** and **elderberries** are most suitable for making jellies and tend to be combined with blander apples, which are higher in pectin, to ensure a good set. **Quinces** are also high in pectin.

EQUIPMENT

It's worth investing in a **preserving pan** because it will last a lifetime – they're wider at the top than the bottom, helping evaporation and allowing a fast-boiling preserve to rise without boiling over. Stainless steel is a good all-rounder or choose copper, although it's not suitable for making pickles and chutneys. A **thermometer** is more useful rather than essential as you can test for a set with a chilled saucer (see the technique section). **Jelly bag** kits are available from cookshops or you can make your own: take two or three layers of scalded muslin, tie each corner to the leg of an upturned stool and put a bowl underneath. Buy pristine **jars** and lids and waxed discs from good cookshops or mailorder companies; old jars and lids can be used again once sterilized. A wide-necked **jam funnel** will stop you making a sticky mess while potting. Vintage-style labels are a pleasing touch, especially if you are planning to give the preserves as gifts or make your own using luggage labels, stamp sets and string.

A BIT OF TECHNIQUE

• Pre-cook fruit in simmering water to soften the flesh and skin and encourage it to release pectin. Add just a splash of water to juicy fruits such as blackberries and currants; hard fruits including apples and quince should almost be covered.

• Warm the sugar in a heatproof bowl in a low oven – this helps it to dissolve more quickly when added to the fruit.

• To see if it has set, pop a few saucers in the freezer to chill, drop a teaspoonful of the jelly or jam onto the saucer and leave for a minute. Push with your finger – if it wrinkles it's set. If it doesn't, keep on boiling and re-testing every couple of minutes.

• Jam containing pieces of fruit should stand for 15 minutes before potting to stop them floating to the top of the jar; as a rule, jellies should be potted immediately unless extra ingredients are added. Seal immediately, then label the jars when completely cold.

• To sterilize jars, lids, seals and funnels, see page 106.

jelly bag

jam funnel

Lavender and lemon jelly

Jellies are a little more versatile than jams: spread them on toast or scones or melt into savoury sauces. Pot this jelly in smaller jars for serving with roast lamb, so that it can be used up in one sitting.

PREPARATION **15 MINUTES PLUS STANDING**
COOKING **1 HOUR**

Makes about 1.75kg (3½lb)
1.75kg (3½lb) crab or Bramley apples
pared rind and juice of 2 large lemons
3 tablespoons lavender flowers
1.8 litres (3 pints) water
warmed sugar (see Tip, below)

1 Roughly chop the apples, peel, core and all – it contains valuable pectin. Put the fruit, lemon rind, juice and 2 tablespoons of the lavender into a large pan with the water. Cover and simmer for 40–50 minutes until tender.
2 Transfer the mixture to a jelly bag and leave to drip into a bowl for at least 4 hours or preferably overnight (use within 24 hours as the pectin levels will decrease). Don't be tempted to touch or squeeze the bag as it will cloud the final jelly – be patient and let it drip slowly.
3 Measure the juice, allowing 450g (14½oz) sugar for every 600ml (1 pint) of juice. Next, bring the juice to the boil in a preserving pan, then add the sugar to dissolve over a low heat.
4 Boil rapidly for about 10 minutes (too long and the jelly will be rubbery). A couple of minutes before you reach setting point (usually at about 8 minutes), turn down the heat to a bubbling boil. A rapid boil will trap lots of air bubbles and spoil the clarity of your jelly. Skim away any scum from the top.
5 Leave to stand for 15–20 minutes until the jelly has thickened slightly. Stir in the remaining lavender – do this too soon and the flowers will float to the top of the jars. Carefully pour the jelly down the inside of the jar to minimize air bubbles. Seal the jars and leave to stand where they are until cold to stop wrinkles forming. Label your jars.

Tip
Sugar will melt more quickly if it is warm when added to liquid. Put the sugar in a heatproof bowl and place in the oven at its lowest setting for 20 minutes until warm but not hot.

Blackberry and apple jam

A traditional combination of ingredients, with flavour coming from the fragrant berries. Throwing in a few under-ripe berries will help with setting.

PREPARATION **15 MINUTES**
COOKING **35 MINUTES**

Makes about 1.75kg (3½lb)
1.25kg (2½lb) blackberries
juice of 2 lemons
400ml (14fl oz) water
650g (1lb 5oz) crab or Bramley apples,
   peeled, cored and roughly chopped
warmed sugar (see Tip, previous recipe)

1 Pick over the blackberries, rinse and then put in a large pan with the juice of 1 lemon and 100ml (3½fl oz) of the water. Cover and simmer for about 10–15 minutes until they are soft.
2 Put the apples in a separate pan with the remaining lemon juice and water. Cover and simmer until soft and pulpy.
3 Blitz the blackberries briefly in a blender or food processor, then push through a sieve to remove the pips. You can skip this stage but most people prefer a pip-free jam.

4 Weigh the blackberry purée and apple pulp and put into a preserving pan with the same weight of sugar. Slowly dissolve the sugar over a low heat, then bring to a rapid boil for 10–20 minutes until setting point is reached – stir from time to time to make sure the fruit isn't catching on the bottom of the pan and adjust the heat if the jam is boiling too vigorously.
5 Once setting point is reached, skim off the scum. Don't throw this away – it's edible, a cook's perk (eat it on toast)! Pot the mixture while still hot into hot sterilized jars or when completely cold into cold jars – never pot while just warm as this could make your jam go mouldy. Seal, then label when completely cold.

Sloe jelly

Traditionally you should wait until the sloes are bletted by the first frost but if you do it's likely that birds or other human foragers will have got there first. Popping them in the freezer first gives the same result.

PREPARATION **15 MINUTES**
COOKING **1 HOUR**

Makes about 1.75kg (3½lb)
1kg (2lb) sloes
2kg (4lb) crab or Bramley apples,
** roughly chopped**
grated zest and juice of 1 lemon
warmed sugar (see Tip, page 116)

1 Put the sloes in a pan with just enough water to cover. Simmer for 30 minutes until soft and pulpy.
2 Simmer the apples, lemon zest and juice in another pan with almost enough water to cover for 40–50 minutes.
3 Strain the fruit in a jelly bag.
4 Measure the juice, allowing 450g (14½oz) sugar per 600ml (1 pint) of juice. Bring the juice to the boil and then dissolve the sugar over a low heat.
5 Boil rapidly until setting point is reached – see Lavender and Lemon Jelly (page 116). Pot immediately and seal.

Victoria plum jam

Victoria plums have a brief season – make them last a little longer by making a batch of this jam to perk you up during the winter months.

PREPARATION **15 MINUTES**
COOKING **50 MINUTES**

Makes about 1.5kg (3lb)
1.5kg (3lb) Victoria plums, halved and
** stoned**
300ml (½ pint) water
1.5kg (3lb) warmed sugar (see page 116)

1 Put the plums into a preserving pan with the water. Simmer for about 20–30 minutes until the skins are soft.
2 Add the sugar, dissolve, then boil rapidly until setting point. Skim away the scum and any bits of skin that have loosened from the plums and pot (see page 117).

Peach and pear jam

Peaches and pears are relatively low in pectin so the high-pectin lemon juice gives them a helping hand to set.

PREPARATION **15 MINUTES**
COOKING **50 MINUTES**

Makes about 2.25kg (4½lb)
1kg (2lb) peaches or nectarines, peeled,
** stoned and roughly chopped**
1kg (2lb) pears, slightly under-ripe,
** peeled, cored and roughly chopped**
125ml (4fl oz) water
grated zest and juice of 4 lemons
2kg (4lb) warmed sugar (see page 116)

1 Put the fruit in a preserving pan with the water and the lemon zest and juice. Simmer for 20–30 minutes until the fruit is tender, but not mushy.
2 Add the sugar and dissolve over a low heat. Boil rapidly until setting point. Leave to stand; pot (see page 117).

Rose-petal jelly

This is an exquisitely coloured jelly with the scent and taste of rose petals.

PREPARATION **20 MINUTES**
COOKING TIME **1 HOUR**

Makes about 1.75kg (3½lb)
1.75kg (3½lb) crab or Bramley apples,
** roughly chopped**
pared rind and juice of 2 large lemons
50g (2oz) rose petals
2.1 litres (3½ pints) water
warmed sugar (see page 116)
1–2 tablespoons rose water (optional)

1 Simmer the apples as for the Lavender and Lemon Jelly recipe (see page 116), minus the lavender, then strain.
2 Remove the white heels from the petals; roughly chop. Put into a small pan with 300ml (½ pint) of the water and 2 teaspoons sugar. Simmer for 10 minutes, then strain through a muslin-lined sieve.
3 Measure the combined juice and continue from step 3 of the Lavender and Lemon Jelly recipe. Carefully taste a little of the jelly – if the flavour is not pronounced enough, stir in a tablespoon or two of rose water. Pot and seal.

Bakewell pudding

Bakewell pudding is traditionally filled with raspberry jam but this version uses Victoria plum jam (see page 118), which has a natural affinity with almonds.

PREPARATION **20 MINUTES PLUS CHILLING**
COOKING **30–35 MINUTES**

Serves 6–8

1 quantity Basic Shortcrust pastry (see page 28)
2 tablespoons Victoria plum jam (see page 118)
25g (1oz) candied peel
3 large eggs
75g (3oz) caster sugar
125g (4oz) unsalted butter, melted
1 teaspoon vanilla extract
75g (3oz) ground almonds
thick double cream, to serve

1 Preheat the oven to 200°C (180°C fan oven/400°F), gas mark 6. Roll out the pastry on a lightly floured worksurface to a thickness of 3mm (⅛ inch). Use to line a 20cm (8 inch) oval 5cm (2 inch) deep pie dish with a 2cm (¾ inch) rim and crimp the edges with a fork. Chill for 30 minutes.

2 Spread the jam over the base of the pastry and scatter with the candied peel.

3 Whisk the eggs and sugar together until fluffy and lighter in colour. Whisk in the butter and vanilla extract and fold in the ground almonds.

4 Pour the mixture into the pastry case and bake in the oven for 10 minutes. Turn down the oven temperature to 180°C (160°C fan oven/350°F), gas mark 4 and cook for another 20–25 minutes until golden. Serve with thick double cream.

Chutney

Chutneys are the easiest preserves to make and one of the most rewarding. They provide instant gratification and a storecupboard full of treasures that only get better with time. We make them in high summer and early autumn because that's when gardens produce bumper crops. But there is nearly always some produce in season to make the basis of a chutney. There is a lot to be said for making a little, often, to furnish your shelves with a variety of relishes. After all, the whole point of chutneys is to charm the tastebuds with spicy, sweet and sour bursts of flavour that flatter the hard cheeses, cold meats, pies, pasties and curries that have come to seem naked without them.

Well-made chutney will keep for several years and improve rather than deteriorate provided that it is well sealed and not exposed to light. But the idea that chutney has to mature for several months before eating stems, I think, from the days before cider and wine vinegars became common enough to take over from harsher malt vinegar. Which leaves only the question of whether to make chutney that is mild and mellow or buzzing with heat and spice. No need to choose. Let's make both.

Chutney shelf-life

Chutneys must be left for at least a month to mature before eating – even slightly longer if you can bear the wait. During that time the vinegar will mellow and the spices will mingle and soften with the fruit and sugar. Store in a cool, dark place and they will keep for a year or two unopened and for about six months in the fridge once opened.

INGREDIENTS

Chutneys are made with **fruit and vegetables** preserved with vinegar, sugar, salt and spices in infinitely variable combinations. In fact, even using the same recipe, it is not easy to get exactly the same result every time. They are wonderfully versatile users-up of almost any fresh fruit, whether ripe or unripe, and many vegetables, especially overgrown **courgettes** and **marrows**. The only proviso is that the produce used should be in good condition, so while it is fine to use **windfall** fruit such as **apples** or **plums**, it is important to discard all parts that are bruised, damaged or mouldy. **Dried fruits** are also traditional in chutneys, adding sweetness and concentrated depth of flavour in the case of **apricots**, **muscatel raisins**, **prunes**, **figs** and **dried cranberries** or **cherries**.

Dark sugars such as demerara and muscovado add colour as well as sweetness. Use refined or paler unrefined varieties to accentuate the flavour and colour of fruits such as plums, peaches or dessert apples.

Inexpensive **malt vinegar** gets the job done. But good-quality **wine** and **cider vinegars** do it even better, producing chutneys that don't need long maturing to be agreeably mellow.

Heat comes from chillies and ginger. In old recipes these **spices** are invariably dried, but both are now readily available in fresh form to give good flavour as well as heat. Most other spices are used dried and work best when bruised and tied loosely in a muslin bag, which is removed from the cooked chutney before it is potted. **Fennel** and **onion seeds** are an exception to this procedure and can be added directly to the chutney without grinding.

EQUIPMENT

A large capacity, wide-mouthed **pan** made of a material that does not react with the acetic acid of vinegar is an absolute requirement. Brass or copper preserving pans are not suitable (the acetic acid in the vinegar will make the chutney taste bitter and will corrode the metal over time). Although a **stainless steel preserving pan** is the ideal, I use a 28cm (11 inch) round **casserole** with a vitreous enamel lining for making chutneys. It's thick base helps to prevent sticking. A **heat-diffusing mat** has the same effect when cooking on a gas hob. **Scales** for measuring ingredients, hankie-sized pieces of **muslin** for wrapping spices and a **long-handled**

wooden spoon to stir the chutney with are all the kit needed. This is a low-tech pastime.

New or recycled **jars** for bottling chutney can be almost any size or shape. The most important thing is to achieve a good seal with **lids** that do not react with vinegar as bare metal does, or allow evaporation as transparent jam pot covers do. Le Parfait-style jars with glass lids and rubber seals work perfectly as do new lids with a non-reactive coating for screw-top jars. A **jam funnel** makes for easy mess-free bottling – don't forget to **label** your efforts. Most chutneys look… well, brown, no matter how distinctive their flavours.

A BIT OF TECHNIQUE

• Haste is the enemy of a good chutney. Chopping fruit and vegetables by hand is more time-consuming than using a mincer or food processor, but the finished chutney rewards the effort in both appearance and texture.

• Undercooking can result in poor texture and flavour.

• Chutney should be jammy in texture and the flavours well-blended in a whole that is more than the sum of its parts. When you think your chutney is ready, draw your wooden spoon across the base of the pan – it should leave a clear channel for the count of three.

• Chutney-making is a fertile field for creative experiment. When I have ripe, well-flavoured fruit to work with – say early season Opal plums, a basket of peaches or distinctively flavoured dessert apples such as russets or coxes – I turn them into mild chutneys that let the taste of the fruit shine in its own right. Then I let rip with the chillies and spices when the chutney is based on unripe fruit or bland vegetables such as squash. Chutneys are pretty obliging, though, so don't be too fussed if the correct ingredients aren't to hand or you don't have quite enough of one thing: dried fruits, sugars, spices and vinegar are interchangeable and the end result will still taste delicious. Besides, no chutney will taste exactly the same each time, which is part of its charm.

• To sterilize jars, lids, seals and funnels, see page 106.

Green tomato chutney

This is lovely with curries and cold meats. I like to assemble all the ingredients in the pan and leave it overnight before starting to cook the chutney the next morning. This allows the sugar and salt to draw juices from the fruit and onions with the result that the pieces keep their shape when cooked and, while fully tender, don't disintegrate into a mush.

PREPARATION **45 MINUTES**
COOKING **ABOUT 2–3 HOURS**

Makes 2 litres (3½ pints)
1.25kg (2½lb) green tomatoes
500g (1lb) apples, cookers or eaters
750g (1½lb) onions
2 fresh red chillies, medium or hot
3 garlic cloves, peeled
a 4cm (1½ inch) piece of fresh ginger, peeled
  and roughly chopped
750ml (1¼ pints) white wine vinegar
1kg (2lb) golden granulated sugar
1 tablespoon salt

1 Chop the tomatoes, discarding any hard core pieces. Peel, core and chop the apples into pieces of roughly the same size. Peel and chop the onions likewise. Put them all into a large non-reactive pan.
2 Halve the chillies and discard the stalks and seeds. Put them in a blender or food processor with the garlic, ginger and a splash of the vinegar. Blend to a loose, smoothish paste and add it to the pan.
3 Add the rest of the vinegar, the sugar and salt. Put the pan over a medium heat and stir frequently until the sugar has dissolved completely. Then cook the mixture down slowly, stirring more frequently as it thickens. When it is well cooked (about 2–3 hours) pot in sterilized jars and seal.

Red tomato and onion seed chutney

This sweet, mild and mellow chutney is lovely with well-flavoured curries, cold cuts of meats and bread and cheese.

PREPARATION **45 MINUTES**
COOKING **ABOUT 2–3 HOURS**

Makes 2 litres (3½ pints)
1.25kg (2½lb) ripe red tomatoes
500g (1lb) apples, cookers or eaters
750g (1½lb) red onions
1 fresh red chilli, medium or hot
1 large garlic clove, peeled
a 2cm (¾ inch) piece of fresh ginger, peeled
  and roughly chopped
750ml (1¼ pints) white wine vinegar
1kg (2lb) golden granulated sugar
1 tablespoon salt
2 tablespoons onion seeds

1 Chop the tomatoes, discarding any hard core pieces. Peel, core and chop the apples into pieces of roughly the same size. Peel and chop the onions likewise. Put them all into a large non- reactive pan.
2 Halve the chilli and discard the stalk and seeds. Put in a blender or food processor with the garlic, ginger and a splash of the vinegar. Blend to a loose, smoothish paste and add it to the large pan.
3 Add the rest of the vinegar, the sugar and salt. Put the pan over a medium heat and stir frequently until the sugar has dissolved completely. Add the onion seeds, then cook the mixture down slowly, stirring more frequently as it thickens. When it is well cooked (about 2–3 hours) pot in sterilized jars and seal.

Red tomato and onion seed chutney

Red onion marmalade

Onion marmalade has a made-in-heaven affinity with creamy blue cheeses and with cold cooked game, poultry, pâtés and terrines. This version of what has become a very popular preserve is mellow and subtle and I can never make enough of it. Be sure the onions are cooked to a silky soft texture before adding the wine and vinegar.

PREPARATION **30 MINUTES**

COOKING **1 HOUR 20 MINUTES**

Makes about 700ml (1 pint 3fl oz)

3 tablespoons light olive oil

700g (1lb 7oz) red onions, very finely sliced

1 teaspoon salt

1 teaspoon freshly ground black pepper

150g (5oz) golden caster sugar

150ml (¼ pint) sherry vinegar

250ml (8fl oz) full-bodied red wine

2 tablespoons fresh, raw beetroot juice or grenadine

1 Heat the oil in a heavy, medium-sized pan. Add the onions, salt, pepper and sugar and stir. Cover and cook over a low heat until the mixture has produced some liquid. Uncover and cook over a gentle heat, stirring from time to time, for about 30 minutes, or until the onions are soft. Don't allow them to brown.

2 Add the vinegar, wine and beetroot juice or grenadine and continue to cook over a slightly higher heat for about 30 minutes, or until thickened a little.

3 Remove from the heat and pot up at once in warm sterilized jars. Cool completely before sealing.

Variation

• Add 1 tablespoon fennel seeds (which are best of all if they are freshly gathered) with the liquid ingredients.

Pear and pumpkin chutney

Pears can be hard, ripe, or best of all a mixture of both, including windfalls if you have them. Any firm fleshed squash variety can be used. Butternut and acorn have good sweet flavours.

PREPARATION **50 MINUTES**

COOKING **ABOUT 2–3 HOURS**

Makes about 2 litres (3½ pints)

1kg ((2lb) pears, peeled, cored and diced

500g (1lb) pumpkin, or butternut squash, peeled, seeded and diced

500g (1lb) onions, roughly chopped

500g (1lb) raisins, chopped if large

2 garlic cloves, peeled

a 5cm (2 inch) piece of fresh ginger, peeled and roughly chopped

750ml (1¼ pints) cider vinegar

500g (1lb) light muscovado sugar

1½ teaspoons salt

1 tablespoon black peppercorns

1 tablespoon allspice

1 Put the chopped pears, squash, onions and raisins into a large non-reactive pan.

2 In a blender or food processor, blend the garlic, ginger and a splash of the vinegar. Blend to a loose, smoothish paste and add it to the pan. Add the rest of the vinegar, the sugar and salt.

3 Bruise the peppercorns and allspice with a pestle and mortar, and tie them loosely in muslin.

4 Put the pan over a low to medium heat and stir frequently until the sugar has dissolved completely and some liquid has been drawn from the fruit and vegetables. Add the spice bag and cook the mixture down slowly, stirring more frequently as it thickens.

5 When it is well cooked (about 2–3 hours) remove the spice bag and pot the chutney in sterilized jars and seal.

Variations

• **Spicy Pear and Pumpkin Chutney**: to add a punch of heat to the chutney, include 2–3 medium to hot fresh chillies, deseeded and roughly chopped in the blender mix of garlic and ginger. Alternatively, add chilli flakes or include dried chillies or flakes in the spice bag.

• Use dried cranberries instead of raisins.

Plum chutney

To accentuate the plum flavour, crack half a dozen of the plum stones to extract the kernels and include these, bruised, with the spices.

PREPARATION **1 HOUR**

COOKING **ABOUT 2–3 HOURS**

Makes 1.5 litres (2½ pints)

1kg (2lb) ripe plums, halved or quartered and stoned

500g (1lb) cooking apples, peeled and chopped

250g (8oz) pitted prunes, chopped

500g (1lb) red onions, chopped

500g (1lb) golden granulated sugar

1 teaspoon salt

750ml (1¼ pints) red wine vinegar

1 tablespoon black peppercorns

10 cloves

10cm (5 inch) cinnamon stick

1 Put the plums, apples, prunes and onions into a large non-reactive pan with the sugar, salt and vinegar.

2 Bruise the peppercorns, cloves, cinnamon and plum stone kernels (if using) with a pestle and mortar, and tie them loosely in muslin.

3 Put the pan over a low to medium heat and stir frequently until the sugar has dissolved completely and some liquid has been drawn from the fruit and vegetables. Add the spice bag and cook the mixture down slowly, stirring more frequently as it thickens.

4 When the chutney is well cooked (about 2–3 hours) remove the spice bag and pot the chutney in sterilized jars and seal.

Green tomato chutney (see page 124)

Red tomato and onion seed chutney (see page 124)

Plum Chutney

Red onion marmalade

Spicy pear and pumpkin chutney

Pear and pumpkin chutney

Pickling

A simple sweet or pungent pickle can be created by packing practically any kind of fruit or vegetable into jars and topping it up with cold vinegar. More elaborate concoctions combine aromatic herbs and fragrant spices with sufficient sugar to both soften the tartness and to improve the flavour and texture, which can range from sour to sweet, crisp to tender. When it comes to eating, patience is essential; the longer the pickle can be left to mature the mellower the final result.

The pickling larder

A larder packed with pickled vegetables and fruit offers infinite possibilities for simple suppers with cold meats and cheese. Sharp, salty or sweet-sour, the most appealing ingredients used are either crunchy, such as red cabbage, onions and gherkins, or sweet like pears, peaches and plums. Subtle but satisfying tweaks can be made with a variety of herbs and spices and different flavoured vinegars.

Pickled Red Cabbage (see page 132)

INGREDIENTS

Vinegar preserves by penetrating food, replacing its natural liquids and inhibiting the growth of micro-organisms. It also infuses the food with its own flavour so the pickle will only ever be as good as the quality of vinegar used. **Wine vinegars** are the finest and create delicate, subtle pickles, but the less expensive **cider**, **malt** and **distilled varieties** also produce delicious, if slightly more robust, results. Check the label to ensure your vinegar has at least 5% acetic acid content for successful preservation.

Sugar is also an important preservative and, depending on the variety, can simply mellow the vinegar or, in the case of **muscovado**, add another dimension to the end result altogether.

Both the vinegar and sugar you choose will affect the final colour: distilled or white wine vinegar and white granulated sugar, for example, are ideal for creating clear pickles, and won't alter the natural colour of pale produce such as cauliflower or eggs.

Subtle use of **herbs** and **spices** take pickles to even higher levels. They can be tied in a muslin bag to infuse during preparation, strained before final pickling or added to the jars for interest. Always use whole spices as ground versions cloud the vinegar.

EQUIPMENT

Happily, pickle making doesn't require specialist equipment. However, all utensils and containers should be **stainless steel**, **glass** or **enamel**, with a **nylon sieve** for straining, because the acid in vinegar reacts with certain metals, turning pickles bitter. **Kilner jars** or **jam jars** with **vinegar-proof lids** make good containers, or traditional **large pickle jars**. Sterilize them in the hottest cycle of your dishwasher or wash in hot, soapy water, then put in the oven at 150°C (130°C fan oven/300°F), gas mark 2 for 20 minutes. The pickles must remain submerged in the vinegar – if they're bobbing above the liquid a disc of **wax paper** will hold them below the surface.

A BIT OF TECHNIQUE

• There are two methods of pickling: hot and cold. For the former, vinegar is brought to the boil with flavourings and poured over vegetables, enabling it to penetrate more quickly and soften them slightly – particularly good for large, firm vegetables, such as beetroot. Alternatively, cold vinegar is simply poured over vegetables, such as cauliflower, to keep them crunchy.

• Salt also plays an important role in pickling techniques because it helps to draw out excess moisture and keep vegetables crisp. Dry salting is used when pickling delicate vegetables such as cucumber. Slices are sprinkled with salt and left for 24 hours. Then they are rinsed, dried and packed into jars with vinegar. As a rule, allow 50g (2oz) salt for each 450g (14½oz) vegetables.

• A brine (wet salting) is used for firmer vegetables, such as pickling onions, and is left for 24 hours before rinsing. Allow 50g (2oz) salt for every 600ml (1 pint) water – it should be buoyant enough to be able to float a fresh egg in it.

Pickled shallots

Shallots have a slightly more delicate flavour than their robust cousins, pickling onions.

PREPARATION **40 MINUTES PLUS STANDING**
COOKING **10 MINUTES**

Makes 1.5kg (3lb)
800g (1lb 9oz) shallots, peeled and trimmed
75g (3oz) sea salt
600ml (1 pint) boiling water
600ml (1 pint) distilled vinegar
175g (6oz) dark brown sugar
1 blade of mace
**½ teaspoon each Sichuan and black peppercorns,
  plus extra for potting**
1 star anise, plus extra for potting
bay leaves, for potting

1 Put the shallots and salt into a large non-metallic bowl and add the boiling water. Cover and leave to stand overnight.
2 Put the remaining ingredients into a pan. Bring to the boil and simmer for 5 minutes.
3 Drain the shallots and add to the pan. Simmer for 5 minutes until transparent but still crisp. Remove with a slotted spoon.
4 Pack sterilized jars two-thirds full with the shallots. Pour over the hot vinegar, adding a few peppercorns to each jar, a star anise and a bay leaf. Store in a cool, dark place for 1 month before eating.

Pickled red cabbage

Serve this vibrantly coloured, crunchy pickle with stews and roast meats, or a good home-cooked slice of cold ham.

PREPARATION **15 MINUTES PLUS SALTING**
COOKING **5 MINUTES**

Makes about 1.5kg (3lb)
1 red cabbage, cored and roughly shredded
sea salt
700ml (1 pint 3fl oz) red wine vinegar
500ml (17fl oz) Raspberry Vinegar (see page 142)
3 large bay leaves
6 cloves
12 juniper berries

1 Layer the cabbage in a bowl, sprinkling with salt as you go. Cover and leave overnight.
2 Rinse the cabbage, pat dry and pack into sterilized jars.
3 Put the remaining ingredients into a pan and boil for about 3 minutes. Pour the vinegar over the cabbage so that it is submerged – just add more vinegar if there isn't enough. Seal and store in a cool, dark place for 1 month before eating.

Fruit mustard pickle

An unusual sweet and hot fruit pickle originating from Northern Italy called *mostarda di frutta*, where it is served with boiled meat, but equally delicious with cured meats.

PREPARATION **30 MINUTES PLUS STANDING**
COOKING **30 MINUTES**

Makes about 1kg (2lb)
850g (1lb 11oz) granulated sugar
150ml (¼ pint) water
125g (4oz) lemons and limes, sliced
250g (8oz) plums, halved and stoned
125g (4oz) black grapes
250g (8oz) melon, cubed or balled
250g (8oz) pineapple
150ml (¼ pint) white wine vinegar
50g (2oz) English mustard powder

1 Put 600g (1lb 3oz) of the sugar into a large pan with the water. Melt over a gentle heat until the sugar is dissolved.
2 Add the fruit and cook over a low heat for 10–15 minutes until it softens slightly. Pour into a bowl.
3 Put the remaining sugar into the pan with the vinegar and simmer for 15 minutes until it is thick and syrupy. Cool.
4 Mix 2 tablespoons of the vinegar with the mustard powder, then stir into the rest of the vinegar. Leave to thicken for 1 hour.
5 Add the mustard vinegar to the fruit, stir well and then pack into warm, sterilized jars. Store in a cool, dark place for 2 weeks before eating.

Spiced oranges

A sweet, spicy pickle that is perfect served with ham. Choose unwaxed oranges if you can find them or scrub thoroughly before cooking to remove the wax coating.

PREPARATION **30 MINUTES PLUS STANDING**
COOKING **1 HOUR 20 MINUTES**

Makes about 1.5kg (3lb)
10 thin-skinned oranges
600ml (1 pint) white wine vinegar
1kg (2lb) granulated sugar
1 large cinnamon stick
4 allspice berries
about 12 cloves

1 Cut the oranges into 5mm (¼ inch) slices. Put in a pan and cover with cold water. Simmer for 30–40 minutes until the peel is tender.
2 Put the remaining ingredients in another pan and heat gently until the sugar is dissolved. Bring to the boil for 2 minutes.
3 Remove the orange slices with a slotted spoon, reserving the poaching liquid, and put into the vinegar mixture. Simmer for 30 minutes until the oranges are translucent. Leave to stand in the liquid overnight.
4 The next day, simmer the oranges again until they are completely tender. Put into sterilized jars and cover with the syrup. Keep the poaching liquid in the fridge and use to top up the orange slices if they absorb some of the vinegar syrup. Store in a cool, dark place for 6 weeks before eating.

Pickled quail eggs

A tasty little snack or accompaniment to curries, these pickled quail eggs are incredibly moreish.

PREPARATION **20 MINUTES PLUS COOLING**
COOKING **5 MINUTES**

Makes about 450g (14½oz)
300ml (½ pint) cider vinegar
a 1.5cm (¾ inch) piece of fresh ginger, sliced
½ tablespoon coriander seeds
2 dried red chillies
½ tablespoon black peppercorns
24 quail eggs

1 Put all the ingredients, except the eggs, in a pan. Bring to the boil, then simmer for 5 minutes. Leave to cool completely.
2 Gently bubble the eggs in simmering water for 2½ minutes until hard-boiled. Cool under cold running water. Peel when cool enough to handle and pack into sterilized jars.
3 Strain the vinegar and pour over the eggs to cover completely. Add a few of the spices for decoration if you like. Seal with vinegar-proof lids. Store in a cool, dark place for 6 weeks before eating,

Aromatic spiced pears

Particularly good with cold meats or cheese. Use firm pears such as Conference or Williams for best results.

PREPARATION **20 MINUTES**
COOKING **ABOUT 30 MINUTES**

Makes about 1kg (2lb)
500g (1lb) granulated sugar
500ml (17fl oz) distilled vinegar
juice and pared rind 1 lemon
1 teaspoon allspice berries
1 teaspoon whole cloves
2 small cinnamon sticks
1.25kg (2½lb) hard pears

1 Put all of the ingredients, except the pears, into a large pan. Heat gently until the sugar is dissolved, then bring to the boil for 5 minutes.
2 Meanwhile, peel and core the pears, slicing into quarters, halves or keeping whole depending on their size.
3 Add the pears to the vinegar mixture and gently poach until just tender – this can take from 5–20 minutes depending on their ripeness. Remove with a slotted spoon as they become tender and transfer to hot, sterilized jars.
4 Boil and reduce the vinegar by a third, then strain over the pears, adding some of the whole spices for decoration. Cover the top of the pears with waxed paper to keep them submerged and seal with a vinegar-proof lid. Store in a cool, dark place for at least 1 month before eating.

Bottling and liqueurs

Capturing the essence of produce picked at the height of perfection, luscious bottled fruits and fresh, clean tasting cordials bring welcome cheer to the table. At harvest time, the country kitchen would traditionally be a hive of activity, turning home-grown and foraged food into a stock of delicious storecupboard treats for long winter days. Sadly, this thrifty practice has fallen out of favour since the advent of freezers, but deserves to be revived. Not only does it have a virtue of economy by preserving goods when at their most abundant, but it also tastes far superior to anything similar purchased out of season.

Bottling

Whether it's harvesting an orchard glut of fruit, infusing the flavour of delicate herbs in oil or vinegar or capturing the deep savoury flavour of mushrooms in a ketchup, there is still a place for bottling in the modern country kitchen. Preserving by this method isn't complicated if the simple rules are followed. Most agreeably for the cook, it stocks up the pantry with exciting and versatile food that cheers up the winter table by enabling ingredients to be used out of season with little change to texture and flavour. A touch of forward planning in the warmer months also enables the dedicated cook to use seasonal produce at its peak to make pleasing Christmas gifts for family and friends.

INGREDIENTS

Bottling is a great way of preserving **delicate fruits** that would be damaged by freezing, keeping their texture and flavour similar to their original state.

Fruit should be firm and just ripe and free from bruises. Remove stalks from small fruits such as **redcurrants** and **gooseberries** and leave whole. Larger fruits such as **apricots** and **peaches** are best halved and stoned; blanch and peel away the skins. **Pears** are low in acid so 2 teaspoons lemon juice should be added to every 500ml (17fl oz) sugar syrup before processing.

A **sugar syrup** preserves the colour and texture of the fruit and once the preserve is opened can be drizzled over ice cream or added to drinks. The strength of syrup depends on personal taste but a lighter one is more attractive if the preserve is a gift. For a light sugar syrup, dissolve 125g (4oz) granulated sugar in 600ml (1 pint) water over a low heat, then boil for 2 minutes without stirring; for a medium syrup use 250g (8oz) sugar to 600ml (1 pint) water; for a heavy syrup use 375g (12oz) sugar to 600ml (1 pint) water.

Fruit juice or **alcohol**, such as brandy, gin or vodka, can be substituted for the sugar syrup. **Whole spices** can be added for an extra flavour depth (ground spices will cloud the syrup).

Firm or fibrous fruit such as **apples**, **pears** and **apricots** benefit from pre-cooking in sugar syrup. Toss in lemon juice first to prevent discolouration.

EQUIPMENT

Jars and **bottles** need to be thicker than normal jam jars to withstand the heating process. **Clip jars** have glass lids fitted with rubber rings and a metal clip to seal; **screw-top (Kilner) jars** are sealed with metal lids and a separate metal screw band. A **deep pan** and **thermometer** are necessary if you plan to process the jars using the water bath method, otherwise a large **baking sheet** or **roasting pan** may be used for the oven method.

A BIT OF TECHNIQUE

• All equipment should be scrupulously clean to prevent contamination. Bacteria that cause spoilage are destroyed at temperatures from 74–100°C (165–212°F) and can be reached by heating raw or cooked produce in a simple water bath or in the oven.
• Acidity is key: the more acid the food contains, the more easily the organisms are destroyed by heat. Low acid foods must be preserved at higher temperatures with specialist equipment to prevent bacterial spores causing food poisoning so is not recommended for the home cook.
• Sterilize jars by running on the hottest cycle of your dishwasher or wash in hot, soapy water, then put on a foil-lined baking tray in the oven at 150°C (130°C fan oven/300°F), gas mark 2 for 20 minutes. Sterilize the lids and rubber rings in boiling water.
• To process: fill sterilized jars and put the lids in place. Screw-band lids should be tightened, then unscrewed by a quarter turn. Fit clip jars with the rubber ring and position the clip over the hinge to hold the lid in place if using the oven method or clamp in place if using the water bath technique.
• To process jars or bottles in the oven, space them apart on a newspaper-lined baking sheet. Put in the oven at 150°C (130°C fan oven/300°F), gas mark 2 for the specified time. Remove and tighten the screw lids or clips at once.
• To process jars or bottles in a water bath, space apart on a trivet set in a large, deep pan. Pour in enough warm water to cover the jars by 2.5cm (1 inch). Cover the pan with a lid and slowly bring to a simmer for the required length of time. Remove and tighten the lids or clips immediately.

PROCESSING TIMES

Only foods with a high level of acidity can be processed at home safely. If using the water bath process, warm water must be slowly brought to a particular temperature over 25 minutes and held there for a specified length of time (see chart opposite).

TESTING FOR A SEAL

Leave to stand for 24 hours. The screw-top jars should make a seal as they cool – the lid should look slightly concave. Press the top with a finger and if it pops up, it has not sealed. To test clip jars, undo the clip and try to open the lid with a fingernail; if it remains in place then the seal is airtight. If the seal hasn't worked, store the jar in the fridge and eat the contents within two weeks. Immediately before consuming the contents, check the seal is still effective before opening. If a jar lid ruptures or pops up during storage the contents should be discarded.

Bottled rhubarb with orange and ginger (see page 140)

BOTTLING TIMES

Produce	Oven method (minutes)	Water bath method (minutes and temperature)
Apple slices	30–40	2 @ 74°C (165°F)
Apricots, halved	40–50	20 @ 82°C (180°F)
Blackberries	30–40	2 @ 74°C (165°F)
Blackcurrants	30–40	2 @ 74°C (165°F)
Blueberries	30–40	2 @ 74°C (165°F)
Cherries	40–50	10 @ 82°C (180°F)
Citrus fruit	30–40	10 @ 74°C (165°F)
Cranberries	30–40	2 @ 74°C (165°F)
Gooseberries	40–50	2 @ 74°C (165°F)
Nectarines, halved	50–60	20 @ 82°C (180°F)
Peaches, halved	50–60	20 @ 82°C (180°F)
Pears, halved	60	60 @ 88°C (190°F)
Plums, halved	50–60	20 @ 82°C (180°F)
Quinces, sliced	40–50	30 @ 88°C (190°F)
Raspberries	30–40	2 @ 74°C (165°F)
Redcurrants	30–40	2 @ 74°C (165°F)
Rhubarb	40–50	2 @ 74°C (165°F)
Tomatoes, whole	60–80	50 @ 88°C (190°F)

Bottled clementines

A ready-made sauce for drizzling over pancakes.

PREPARATION **20 MINUTES PLUS PROCESSING**

Makes 1 litre (1¾ pints)
125g (4oz) granulated sugar
600ml (1 pint) water
10–12 clementines
3 cloves
1 small stick cinnamon

1 Dissolve the sugar in the water in a saucepan over a gentle heat, then boil for 2 minutes without stirring to make a sugar syrup. You may not need all of the syrup but it will keep for several weeks in a container in the fridge. Peel the clementines and leave whole. Peel away any white pith.
2 Pack one-third of the fruit into a large sterilized jar and pour in enough hot syrup to cover. Add the cloves and cinnamon. Add another third of the clementines and syrup to cover. Repeat until all the fruit is used ensuring there is a 2.5cm (1 inch) gap at the top. Completely cover the fruit with syrup.
3 Seal the jar and heat process in a water bath for 10 minutes at 74°C (165°F) or in the oven for 30–40 minutes (see page 138).
4 Check the seal before storing in a cool, dark place. Store in the fridge once opened and use within 1 month.

Bottled rhubarb with orange and ginger

Drizzle the juices over ice cream or use in cocktails.

PREPARATION **20 MINUTES PLUS PROCESSING**

Makes 700ml (1 pint 3fl oz)
250g (8oz) granulated sugar
600ml (1 pint) water
juice of 1 large orange
450g (14½oz) rhubarb
a 2cm (¾ inch) piece of fresh ginger, peeled and sliced

1 Dissolve the sugar in the water in a saucepan over a gentle heat, then boil for 2 minutes without stirring to make a sugar syrup. Stir in the orange juice.
2 Slice the rhubarb into chunks and pack it into sterilized jars along with the sliced ginger.
3 Pour over the hot sugar syrup to cover. Seal the jar and heat process in a water bath for 2 minutes at 74°C (165°F) or in the oven for 40–50 minutes (see page 138).
4 Check the seal before storing in a cool, dark place. Store in the fridge once opened and use within 1 month.

Cherries in brandy

Most soft fruits can be bottled in alcohol and because the spirit acts as a preservative there is no need to heat process the sterilized jars after sealing.

1 Prick each cherry with a needle. You can remove the stones from the fruit, or not, as you like. Pack the cherries into a sterilized, wide-necked, preserving jar with the spices.
2 Add the sugar to the jar and pour over the brandy. Seal and gently turn the jar to help dissolve the sugar.

3 Store in a cool, dark place for 2 months before eating, turning once a week for the first month to ensure the sugar is dissolved. The longer you leave the fruit to mature the better they will taste. Store in the fridge once opened and use within 6 months.

PREPARATION **15 MINUTES**

Makes 1kg (2lb)
1kg (2lb) sweet cherries
6 cloves
1 cinnamon stick
1 blade of mace
about 750ml (1¼ pints) brandy
350g (11½oz) granulated sugar

Basil oil

A few sprigs of rosemary, thyme or tarragon could replace the basil.

PREPARATION **10 MINUTES PLUS STANDING**

Makes 600ml (1 pint)
a handful basil leaves
600ml (1 pint) olive oil

1 Put the ingredients into a large jar or bowl making sure the herbs are submerged. Cover with a lid or cling film and leave in a cool, dark place for 1 month, swirling occasionally.
2 Strain the oil into sterilized bottles. Add a herb sprig if you like and seal. Store in a cool, dry place for up to 6 months.

Tarragon vinegar

This is an essential ingredient for a classic béarnaise sauce.

PREPARATION **10 MINUTES PLUS STANDING**

Makes 500ml (17fl oz)
3 large sprigs fresh tarragon
500ml (17fl oz) white wine vinegar

1 Put the ingredients into a large jar or bowl making sure the herbs are submerged. Cover with a lid or cling film and leave in a cool, dark place for 2 weeks, swirling occasionally.
2 Strain the vinegar into sterilized bottles. Add a herb sprig for decoration if you like and seal. Store in a cool, dry place for up to 1 year.

Raspberry vinegar

If fresh raspberries are out of season, use defrosted frozen raspberries.

PREPARATION **10 MINUTES PLUS STANDING**

Makes about 750ml (1 ¼ pints)
500g (1lb) fresh raspberries
600ml (1 pint) white wine vinegar

1 Lightly mash the raspberries in a non-metallic bowl, then stir in the vinegar. Cover the bowl with cling film and leave in a cool, dark place for 1 week.
2 Strain the mixture through muslin into a bowl or jug, then decant into sterilized bottles with a funnel. Seal and label. Store in a cool place for up to 1 year.

Flavoured oils and vinegars are quick to make and don't need to be heat processed. Use them in dressings, stir-fries and when marinating meat, fish and vegetables.

Chilli oil

Be aware that chillies vary in their hotness but if you want a very fiery oil you can add the seeds too.

PREPARATION **10 MINUTES PLUS STANDING**

Makes 600ml (1 pint)
9 fresh or dried whole chillies
600ml (1 pint) sunflower oil

1 Halve and deseed the fresh chillies or split the dried chillies. Pack them into a large jar or bowl and pour over the oil. Cover with a lid or cling film and leave in a cool, dark place for 2 weeks.
2 When it has reached the desired level of hotness, strain the oil into sterilized bottles. Add a dried chilli for decoration if you like and seal. Store in a cool, dry place for up to 6 months.

Tomato ketchup

Choose very ripe, red tomatoes for the best flavour.

PREPARATION **30 MINUTES**
COOKING **2½–3¾ HOURS**

Makes 1 litre (1¾ pints)
3kg (6lb) very ripe tomatoes, chopped
2 onions, chopped
1 green pepper, deseeded and chopped
125g (4oz) soft light brown sugar
175ml (6fl oz) distilled vinegar
½ tablespoon paprika
½ tablespoon dry mustard powder

FOR THE SPICE BAG
1 small cinnamon stick
3 black peppercorns
3 allspice berries
6 cloves
½ teaspoon fennel seeds

1 Put the tomatoes, onions and green pepper in a saucepan and cook for 30–40 minutes over a low heat until soft. Blitz in a blender or food processor, then push through a sieve into a bowl.
2 Tie the whole spices in a piece of muslin to make a spice bag.
3 Put the puréed tomatoes in a large saucepan and add the remaining ingredients and the spice bag. Simmer, covered, for 2–3 hours until thickened but still pourable.
4 Remove the spice bag and pour the tomato mixture into sterilized bottles, leaving a 2.5cm (1 inch) gap at the top. Heat process in a water bath for 30 minutes at 84°C (183°F) or in the oven for 50 minutes (see page 138).
5 Store in a cool, dark place and in the fridge once opened. Use within 2 months.

Mushroom ketchup

Add a dash to casseroles and pie mixtures for extra depth of flavour.

PREPARATION **30 MINUTES**
COOKING **1½–2 HOURS**

Makes about 750ml (1¼ pints)
900g (1¾lb) mushrooms, finely chopped
1 pack dried wild mushrooms, about 30g (1oz)
¼ teaspoon ground cloves
½ teaspoon ground mace
½ teaspoon ground allspice
2 anchovy fillets
300ml (½ pint) Madeira
75ml (3fl oz) water

1 Put all of the ingredients into a large saucepan with the water and bring to the boil. Simmer very gently, uncovered, for 1 hour.
2 Strain the mushrooms through a muslin-lined sieve into a bowl, squeezing out as much juice as possible.
3 Return the liquid to the saucepan and boil to reduce over a medium heat to the consistency you prefer – thicker for a condiment, thinner if to be used as a flavouring for soups and stocks etc.
4 Pour into sterilized bottles and store in a cool, dark place for 3 months. Refrigerate once opened and use within 6 months. To extend the life of the ketchup for up to 1 year, process with the water bath method to 100°C (212°F) for 20 minutes or in the oven for 50 minutes (see page 138).

Liqueurs and cordials

Homemade cordials and liqueurs
are luxurious additions to the country pantry, often
made with the most frugal of ingredients. Flowers
and berries can be transformed into delightful
summer drinks or cordials, while a warming
liqueur made from sloes cheers up the darkest of
winter nights and makes a welcome Christmas gift.
Homemade liqueurs and cordials need few special
tools. Squares of muslin will ensure the cordial
is properly strained or a jelly bag can be used for
extra-clear results. A plastic funnel means not a
drop of liquid will be spilled when filling bottles.
Glass bottles, either fitted with corks or swing
stoppers, make attractive containers especially if
the cordial or liqueur is to be a gift.

Blackcurrant cordial

Elderflower cordial

Cranberry and orange vodka

Plum brandy

Sloe or damson brandy

Whisky liqueur

A bit of technique

Pricking fruit helps to release the juice that flavours the alcohol. Always fill the jar or bottle to the top as any air space causes the liqueur's flavour to dissipate. Keeping the drinks in a cool, dark place prolongs their life and, properly stored, liqueurs will keep for many years and improve with age. Extend the life of cordials for up to a year using the water bath or oven method described on page 138.

Elderflower cordial

Pick elderflowers early in the season for the best flavour

PREPARATION **10 MINUTES PLUS STANDING**

Makes about 1 litre (1¾ pints)
900g (1¾lb) granulated sugar
800ml (1¹/3 pints) boiling water
40g (1½oz) citric acid
juice of 2 lemons
12–15 elderflower heads

1 Dissolve the sugar in a large bowl with the water. Stir in the citric acid and lemon juice.
2 Shake the elderflowers to remove any insects, add to the sugar syrup, cover and stand for 5 days, stirring daily.
3 Strain through a muslin-lined sieve. Decant into sterilized bottles. It will keep for up to 1 year in the fridge. Dilute with water, tonic or soda water.

Blackcurrant cordial

Try making this cordial with redcurrants as an alternative.

PREPARATION **10 MINUTES**
COOKING **5 MINUTES**

Makes about 500ml (17fl oz)
450g (14½oz) ripe blackcurrants
150ml (¼ pint) water
granulated sugar

1 Put the berries in a pan with the water and cook lightly for 5 minutes, squashing the fruit with a wooden spoon to extract as much juice as possible.
2 Push through a muslin-lined sieve to extract as much juice as possible. Measure and allow 350g (11½oz) sugar for every 500ml (17fl oz) juice.
3 Dissolve the sugar with the juice over a low heat, then pour into sterilized bottles. Store in the fridge for up to 2 weeks or process in a water bath for 2 minutes at 74°C (165°F) or in the oven for 30–40 minutes (see page 138).

Plum brandy

Eat the plums with ice cream once the liqueur is strained.

PREPARATION **20 MINUTES PLUS STANDING**

Makes about 700ml (1 pint 3fl oz)
700ml (1 pint 3fl oz) brandy
400g (13oz) plums, pierced a few times with a skewer
300g (10oz) granulated sugar

1 Put the ingredients into a large sealable jar.
2 Store in a cool, dark place, turning gently every day for the first week to help the sugar to dissolve. Leave for 1 month to mature.
3 Strain through a muslin-lined sieve into a bowl. Decant into sterilized bottles, seal and label.

Whisky liqueur

An infusion of sugar and spices softens even the harshest whisky into a warming liqueur.

PREPARATION **20 MINUTES PLUS STANDING**

Makes about 700ml (1 pint 3 fl oz)
700ml (1 pint 3fl oz) whisky
thinly pared rind of 1 orange
6 cloves
150g (5oz) dried figs, roughly chopped
100g (3½oz) soft light brown sugar

1 Put the ingredients into a large sealable jar.
2 Store in a cool, dark place, turning gently every day for the first week to help the sugar to dissolve. Leave for 1 month to mature.
3 Strain through a muslin-lined sieve into a bowl. Decant into sterilized bottles, seal and label.

Cranberry and orange vodka

The flavours of Christmas in a glass.

PREPARATION **20 MINUTES PLUS STANDING**

Makes about 1 litre (1¾ pints)
1 litre (1¾ pints) vodka
thinly pared rind of 1 orange
275g (9oz) granulated sugar
100g (3½oz) dried cranberries
1 small cinnamon stick

1 Put the ingredients into a large sealable jar.
2 Store in a cool, dark place, turning gently every day for the first week to help the sugar to dissolve. Leave for 1 month to mature.
3 Strain through a muslin-lined sieve into a bowl. Decant into sterilized bottles, seal and label.

Sloe or damson brandy

Of course, you can replace the brandy with the more traditional gin if you prefer.

PREPARATION **15 MINUTES**

Makes about 900ml (1½ pints)
450g (14½oz) sloes or damsons
200g (7oz) caster sugar
700ml (1 pint 3fl oz) brandy

1 Prick the sloes or damsons with a needle a few times. Put into a large wide-necked jar.
2 Add the sugar and brandy and stir well. Strain through a muslin-lined sieve into a bowl. Decant into sterilized bottles, seal and label. Store in a cool, dark place for 3 months, shaking gently once a week.

Sloe brandy, ginger and apple punch

Serve this refreshing long drink with plenty of ice, mint sprigs and lemon slices.

PREPARATION **10 MINUTES**

Makes about 2.5 litres (4 pints)
500ml (17fl oz) sloe brandy (see previous recipe)
1 litre (1¾ pints) dry ginger ale
1 litre (1¾ pints) fresh apple juice
juice of 1 lemon
2 tablespoons caster sugar

1 Mix all of the ingredients together and serve at once.

Sloe brandy, ginger and apple punch

Lemon barley water

Make an orange barley water with two oranges instead.

PREPARATION **20 MINUTES PLUS STANDING**
COOKING **5 MINUTES**

Makes 1.5 litres (2½ pints)
125g (4oz) pearl barley
50g (2oz) granulated sugar
pared rind and juice of 4 large unwaxed lemons
1.1 litres (1¾ pints) boiling water

1 Rinse the pearl barley in several changes of cold water until it runs clear.
2 Put the pearl barley in a pan and cover with cold water. Bring to the boil, then simmer for 5 minutes. Drain and rinse in cold water.
3 Put the pearl barley in a large bowl with the sugar, lemon rind and the boiling water. Stir to dissolve the sugar, then cover and leave to infuse until cold.
4 Strain the pearl barley through a muslin-lined sieve. Stir in the lemon juice and chill. Store in the fridge and use within 3 days.

Ginger beer

Once the ginger has fermented, drink within a couple of days.

PREPARATION **20 MINUTES PLUS STANDING**

Makes about 4.5 litres (7¾ pints)
a 5cm (2 inch) piece of fresh ginger
15g (½oz) cream of tartar
450g (14½oz) granulated sugar
rind and juice of 1 lemon
4 litres (7 pints) boiling water
15g (½oz) fresh yeast or 7g (¼oz)
  dried yeast

1 Roughly slice the ginger and put into a large bowl with the cream of tartar, sugar and lemon rind. Pour in the boiling water. Stir until the sugar is dissolved. Leave to stand until hand hot.
2 Add the lemon juice and yeast. Cover and leave in a warm place for 24 hours.
3 Skim and strain the liquid through muslin into sterilized swing-stoppered glass bottles.
4 Leave for 2–3 days, checking daily to make sure the ginger beer is not too fizzy – loosen the caps if the liquid looks too fizzy to avoid the bottles exploding. Store in the fridge and use within 3 days.

Curing
and potting

In times past, preserving food was a matter of survival. When the cottager's pig was slaughtered in winter, the meat was hung high up in the chimney to smoke, or transformed into sausages and cured salamis. Fresh fish was smoked, salted or potted to extend its life and make it unappealing to bacteria. Translucent slices of smoked salmon, magnificent hams and the finest bacon all owe their tantalizingly complex flavours to these traditional practices. Now, with fridges and freezers to take care of safe storage, we can explore what they have to offer simply for our own pleasure.

Salting

Country cooks once preserved the family pig in layers of salt to ensure a supply of meat for the winter. Before refrigeration it was the simplest and most widespread technique for preserving food. Although quick and reliable, the meat did need thorough soaking for days on end to make it edible. Consequently, flavour became important too and this technique evolved to include sugar, herbs and spices in the salting mixtures. Modern methods of preservation have rendered salting unnecessary and it is now carried out for flavour alone. But the processes of dry-salting and wet-salting (brining) are simple enough to do in your own kitchen and the results are always pleasing. Dry-salting is the most straightforward and gives quick results: fresh meat or fish is rubbed with a salt mixture and turned every few days. Cheaper cuts of beef respond particularly well to wet salting, transforming its texture and flavour, while a side of fresh salmon becomes a very special treat for large gatherings or celebrations via dry-salting. A few bags of salt and sugar, a sprinkling of aromatic herbs and spices and some fresh fish, meat or vegetables are all you need to create your own very special Gravadlax (see pages 156–157), Salt Beef (see pages 160–161) or Dill Pickles (see page 158).

INGREDIENTS

Salt preserves food by drawing out moisture and dissolving in this liquid, preventing growth of potentially harmful micro-organisms. Use **sea salt** rather than table salt as the latter contains additives that can cause food to discolour. A **dry salt mix** or **brine solution** (see opposite) can be flavoured with **herbs** and **whole spices**. Allspice, mace, pepper, cloves, juniper berries or coriander add character. Sugar, honey or black treacle adds sweetness and depth of flavour. A small amount of **saltpetre** (potassium nitrate or sodium nitrate) can be stirred into the brine or added to the dry salt mix. This was necessary before refrigeration to augment the preserving process – but this merely makes meat look a more appetizing pink rather than a grey colour and isn't strictly necessary nowadays. Some research claims that large amounts of saltpetre can be dangerous so use no more than the minimum effective amount: 10g (¼oz) to every 500g (1lb) salt and 5kg (11lb 4oz) meat. If you do use saltpetre, ensure that you rub some sugar over the meat first: even small amounts of saltpetre can harden the flesh and the sugar will keep it soft.

Meat (beef, pork and gammon), **poultry** (chicken and turkey), **fish** (salmon, fresh anchovies, herrings) and **vegetables** and some **fruits** are suitable for salting. Certain vegetables produce natural lactic bacteria that reacts with salt and ferments (lacto-fermentation); sauerkraut is a good example of this.

EQUIPMENT

Very little equipment is needed but any that is used should be scalded with boiling water first to sterilize. A **plastic bucket** or large non-metallic or enamel **container** is good for holding joints of meat and whole fish in brine. To enable the brine to penetrate large pieces of meat more effectively, pierce the meat all over with a **skewer** or **trussing needle**. Smaller food items can be cured in the fridge sitting in a **lipped tray** to catch drips while larger items in brine that can't be chilled should be stored in a cold, airy environment – a north-facing pantry or garage is ideal – but this is best done during the cooler months of the year. The ideal temperature is 2–7°C (36–45°F) – low enough to discourage bacterial growth but high enough to enable the salt and juices to mingle and flavour the meat. The longer the food is left to cure, the stronger the final flavour will be: for meat this can be anything from 2–4 weeks and with more delicate fish, 2–7 days.

A BIT OF TECHNIQUE

There are two basic methods of preserving food with salt: dry-salting and brining.
• **Dry-salting** involves rubbing salt evenly into food to draw out moisture, which produces a brine. It's most suitable for less bulky cuts so that the salt penetrates rapidly, preventing decay: choose thin pieces of food that can absorb salt quickly, such as vegetables, fish fillets like salmon or small whole fish such as anchovies.
• Larger pieces of food such as beef brisket or gammon can be submerged in a **brine solution**. The brine must be strong enough to extract the juices from the food: a 20% salt solution is ideal. It is strong enough if a fresh egg floats on the surface – if it doesn't, keep adding a little more salt until this happens. When salting vegetables, the ingredients must be kept submerged for the fermentation to succeed. You may need to top up the liquid from time to time: make up a light brine of 15g (½oz) salt mixed with 1 litre (1¾ pints) waters for this purpose.
• Any fish or meat thicker than 5cm (2 inches) is more easily cured by the brining (wet-salting) method.
• Some dishes such as spiced beef are rubbed with salt and spices and left for 2–4 weeks to cure. It is then rinsed and cooked before being ready to eat.
• Fish fillets should be pinboned before curing: gently run your hand over the flesh to feel for bones, then remove any you find with a pair of tweezers.

AN ALL-PURPOSE WET CURE (BRINE)

This brine mix is suitable for most large joints of meat or poultry, even turkey. Make sure that you have enough brine to completely submerge the meat by at least 2cm (5 inches) – see picture right. Keep it in place with a plate weighed down with weights or cans. Some of the water can be replaced with beer, cider or perry if you prefer.

Put 4 litres (7 pints) water into a large pan with 750g (1½lb) coarse salt, 500g (1lb) light muscovado sugar, 10g (¼oz) saltpetre (if using), 2 bay leaves, a large sprig of thyme, 10 crushed peppercorns and 5 crushed allspice berries. Bring to the boil for 5 minutes. Cool completely before using.

An all-purpose wet cure (brine)

Gravadlax

This is perfect served with thin slices of brown bread and butter and a mustard sauce.

PREPARATION **20 MINUTES PLUS SALTING**

Serves 12
1.5kg (3lb) salmon, filleted in 2 pieces
2 tablespoons granulated sugar
1 tablespoon sea salt
1 tablespoon dill, finely chopped
1 tablespoon gin
8 juniper berries, crushed

1 Choose fillets from the thickest part of the salmon if you can and pinbone if necessary. Put one fillet skin-side down on a large board.
2 Mix together the sugar and salt and spread over the salmon flesh. Sprinkle all over with the dill and the gin and juniper berries, making sure it is evenly covered.
3 Place the other fillet on top, skin-side up. Wrap the fillets up tightly with a large piece of foil. Put in a lipped tray or dish and put another tray or plate on top. Weigh it down with weights or large tins. Put in the fridge for 2–3 days or up to 1 week, turning every 12 hours.
4 To serve, slice very thinly and enjoy with soured cream and mustard sauce and slices of brown bread and butter.

Dill pickles

Layer with salt beef for a classic sandwich (see page 161).

PREPARATION **15 MINUTES PLUS MATURING**

Makes about 1kg (2lb)
6 pickling cucumbers, sliced
a few sprigs dill
12 black peppercorns
1 teaspoon celery seeds
25g (1oz) sea salt
600ml (1 pint) water

1 Layer the cucumber, dill, peppercorns and celery seeds in a large sterilized preserving jar.
2 Put the salt in a pan with the water and heat until dissolved. Bring to the boil.
3 Pour enough of the salted boiling water over the cucumber to cover completely. Seal and leave to mature in a cool, dark place for 6 weeks before eating. Store in the fridge once opened and use within 2 months.

Preserved lemons

These lemons can be used in tagines, stews, salads and salsas. Rinse off the brine first and scoop out the flesh, which will be too salty to eat – the softened, edible lemon skin is all you need to impart flavour.

PREPARATION **15 MINUTES PLUS MATURING**

Makes 1kg (2lb)
7 large thin-skinned unwaxed lemons
100g (3½oz) sea salt

1 Holding a lemon over a bowl to catch the juice, cut almost lengthways into quarters, leaving the pieces joined at one end. Remove any pips you can see. Pack about 1 tablespoon salt into the cuts, then close up the lemon. Put into a sterilized, wide-necked preserving jar. Repeat with 5 more lemons, packing them tightly into the jar.
2 Juice the remaining lemon and pour into the jar. Sprinkle with any leftover salt and top up with boiling water, ensuring the lemons are covered. Seal and store in a cool, dark place for 1 month before using. Store in the fridge once opened for up to 1 year.

Baked chicken with preserved lemons

Add a few preserved lemons to a simple one-pan chicken roast dinner for extra depth of flavour.

PREPARATION **20 MINUTES**
COOKING **50 MINUTES**

Serves 4

1 tablespoon olive oil
8 chicken portions, such as thighs and drumsticks
1 Preserved Lemon (see previous recipe), cut into quarters
1 whole garlic bulb, halved
a small bunch of lemon thyme
salt and freshly ground black pepper

1 Heat the oven to 200°C (180°C fan oven/400°F), gas mark 6. Heat the oil in a large hob-proof roasting pan. Brown the chicken pieces all over.

2 Squeeze the preserved lemons over the browned chicken pieces. Tuck the lemon shells, garlic and thyme among the chicken in the roasting pan. Season with salt and freshly ground black pepper.

3 Cook in the oven for 40–45 minutes until the chicken pieces are golden and cooked through.

Salt beef

Delicious served sliced in rye bread with Dill Pickles (see page 158) and plenty of mustard. Store in the fridge for up to 2 weeks.

1 Put all of the ingredients in a large preserving pan, except the meat. Add the cold water and stir to dissolve the sugar and salt. Bring to the boil, then leave to cool completely.

2 Pierce the beef all over with a skewer and put it into a large container or plastic bucket. Pour over the brine. Weigh it down with a plate topped with tins or weights – the meat should remain submerged. Transfer the container to a cold place for 10 days, checking daily to ensure the meat is still at least 2cm (¾ inch) under the surface of the brine.

3 Discard the brine, rinse the beef under cold running water and put it in a large pan. Cover with cold water, bring to the boil, then simmer for 1 hour.

4 Drain, cover with fresh water and simmer again for 1 hour. Repeat once more until the beef is extremely tender. Serve hot or leave to cool in the liquid before slicing if serving cold.

PREPARATION **20 MINUTES PLUS SALTING**
COOKING **3 HOURS**

Serves 8–10
500g (1lb) coarse sea salt
400g (13oz) dark brown sugar
1 tablespoon juniper berries, lightly crushed
2 teaspoons allspice berries
2 fresh bay leaves
4 litres (7 pints) cold water
2kg (4lb) beef brisket

Cold smoking

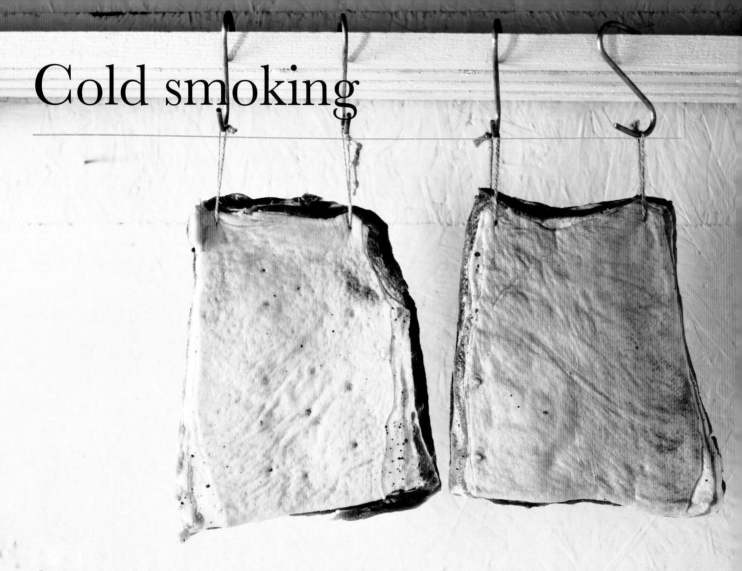

Cold smoking can transform an otherwise bland food to a delicious treat. Unlike hot smoking, which cooks as well as flavours food, cold smoke works its taste-transforming magic at temperatures too low to cook even the fragile flesh of fish.

In times past, preserving food without refrigeration was a matter of survival, so certainty was more important than subtlety. When the cottager's pig was slaughtered in winter, the hams, bacon sides and much else, were immediately salted down, and later dried or hung high up in the chimney to smoke. The salt drew moisture from the meat, dehydrating it and making it unappealing to bacteria. Smoking dried it more and added the inimitable aromas of the wood fire. Well made, bacon and hams remained wholesome for months on end, and were often very salty indeed and dry, which is why so many old recipes begin with instructions for a long soak in cold water.

Try soaking a modern mass-produced ham and you'll be lucky if it tastes of anything much by the time it reaches the plate. Industrial practices designed to speed the curing and smoking of factory-farmed meat and fish – such as injecting brine into bacon, which results in the notoriously unpopular white goo in the frying pan – have fuelled the success of artisan producers who rely on more traditional methods and livestock.

Smoking is usually described as an art. At the domestic level it is more folk-art than science and its recipes offer what seem at first to be puzzlingly differing formulas for making, say, streaky bacon or smoked trout. Ingenious people in many places and times and climates, people with different needs and tastes and raw materials, have developed innumerable ways to cure and smoke their produce. It is reassuring to discover that so many different ways of doing things work so well.

INGREDIENTS

Read around the subject of curing and you will find passionate opinions and not a lot of science on the merits of **sea** versus **rock salt**. Organic sea salt is as good as salt gets for flavour and I am lucky to have found a local shop that helpfully gets in 25kg (50lb) bags to order. Whether sea salt or rock salt, the main thing is that it should be as pure as possible. Cooking salt has some additives but is a better bet than table salt, which usually has more.

Sugar's role in curing is to offset the hardening effect of the salt as well as to add flavour. The darker the sugar the stronger its effect on the flavour and colour of the meat. There are sweet cures where the proportion of sugar to salt goes as high as fifty–fifty – much too sweet for my taste, but maybe just what you have been looking for.

A number of smokers use **briquettes** supplied by their manufacturer. **Sawdust** and **woodchips** can be bought from suppliers of smokers, and once you know what works well you can look around for a supply of cheap or free wood waste from local sources. **Oak** and **fruitwoods** are prime smoking materials. **Pine** and other **conifers** should be avoided as the wood gives too strong a taint to the smoke.

EQUIPMENT

There is a lot of inexpensive fun to be had creating a **cold smoker** out of a discarded fridge or filing cabinet and joining it to a source of smoke by a length of tumble dryer venting hose. And there are tried and tested designs for **wooden or brick-built smokehouses** joined by a subterranean trench or trunking to a fire-pit, or made tall enough to cool the smoke as it rises. The challenge they all depend upon is how to keep the smoke-producing woodchips or sawdust smouldering for more than two or three hours at a stretch. So, if you are more interested in food production than in a construction project, buy a smoker. An internet search should bring up a fairly wide choice. As much by luck as good judgement, I chose the **West Country Cold Smoker**. It has a simple yet sophisticated smoke box that burns reliably for eight hours and, in favourable conditions, for as long as 14 hours on one fill of sawdust. It is big enough to smoke a ham, or four pork bellies, or eight sides of salmon, or a dozen trout. There are also **stacking racks** for smoking small stuff, such as eggs or nuts, and anything that is better smoked lying down than hanging up.

A BIT OF TECHNIQUE

• When cold smoking, the temperature should be kept around 26°C (79°F) and below 29°C (84°F) – any higher and you risk the fish disintegrating.
• Brining or dry-salting prior to smoking will firm flesh and improve flavour. It also removes moisture thereby discouraging bacteria. Fish only needs a short brining period from 30 minutes to 2–3 hours depending on the size and how salty you'd like it to taste ultimately.
• To prepare fish for a cold smoker, split from head to tail along the spine. Remove the head and scrape away the gut. Rinse thoroughly, then brine. Leave to drip-dry for a couple of hours before smoking. Ensure that as much surface area of the flesh should be exposed to the smoke – the simplest way is to fix the fish tied back to back on nails studded on wooden poles. Allow sufficient space between them to let smoke circulate freely. If you buy a smoker kit, it will contain hanging racks for the fish (see right). Smaller fish, such as sardines, are best smoked on a mesh tray.
• Smoke small fish for 3–6 hours and larger, fattier fish for 6–10 hours. However, experimentation is the key to smoking. Make copious notes of what you do at each stage so that you can repeat or adjust the process every time to your liking.
• Once smoking is complete, leave the fish in a cool place before chilling. Smoked foods will keep in the fridge for at least a week and can also be frozen.

A hanging rack of smoking trout (see page 168)

Dry-cured, smoked organic streaky bacon

Dry-cured, smoked organic streaky bacon is hard to find in one piece and is not difficult to make. It is invaluable as a basis for substantial soups, casseroles and bean dishes, and makes crisp breakfast rashers.

When bacon was made without refrigeration, copious quantities of salt were used to cure it and often saltpetre was added as an additional precautionary preservative, which had the side-effect of making the bacon prettily pink. Although it is a permitted preservative, saltpetre (E252, potassium nitrate) has form as a carcinogen, and its use is now tightly controlled. But there is a modern alternative. Ready-made mixtures of curing salts (see page 192) containing small quantities of E250, sodium nitrite and E251, sodium nitrate, also produce rosy pink bacon and ham. They are used in smaller quantities than the recipe that follows, and the curing stage is generally done in vacuum packs under refrigeration. All this is eminently achievable on a domestic scale but does require a vacuum-packing machine.

How salty do you like your bacon? Do you prefer it lightly smoked or pretty pervasive? These are questions of individual taste, and this is where practice pays off. Keep a notebook and learn from your trials and triumphs.

CURING **4–7 DAYS** DRYING **24–48 HOURS**
SMOKING **24–48 HOURS**

Makes about 5.5kg (11lb)
8kg (16lb) thin end belly of pork, boned and not scored (about 3 or 4 pieces)
2kg (4lb) coarse sea salt
500g (1lb) demerara sugar
100g (3½oz) juniper berries, crushed (optional)

1 The salted meat will produce copious amounts of liquid and is better raised above this than left sitting in it. Find a plastic box that will hold the pork bellies in a stack and make a few holes around the edge of the base. Set this box in a larger plastic box, raising it a short way off the bottom. Ideally the larger box will have a lid. Note the weight of the pork pieces, together or separately. When they are cured and smoked they may have lost up to 30% of their weight.

2 Mix the salt, sugar and juniper berries thoroughly together. Strew a layer of the salt mixture over the base of the smaller box. Rub a handful of the salt mixture into both sides of the first piece of pork and lay it, flesh side down, in the box. Add the remaining pieces of pork, rubbing the salting mixture into each one before adding it to the stack, and ending with a layer of salt. There will be salt left over.

3 Cover the meat and put the box somewhere cool and dark – a cold larder, garage or the bottom of the fridge. After 2 days, drain off the liquid in the lower box and repack the meat, with a little more of the curing mix, rearranging the pieces so that the top one goes to the bottom of the stack and so on.

4 Drain and repack the meat daily for another 2 days, making 5 days curing in all, by which time the salt should have penetrated to the centre of the meat. If

the bellies are a bit skinny reduce this by 1 day, and if they are very thick and fat, or the weather is particularly cold, add 1–2 days.

5 Now rinse off the salt cure and hang up the bellies to dry in a cool, airy spot for 24–48 hours. You now have green bacon. When the surface is dry, and a little tacky, it is ready to smoke.

6 Fire up the smoker and hang the bacon pieces in the smoke, making sure that they are not touching each other or the sides. In an ideal world, the temperature in the smoke chamber will be in the 21–32°C (70–90°F) range. Smoke the bacon for 24–48 hours. In cold or very damp weather the smoke penetrates more slowly.

7 You now have smoked bacon. If you can bear the suspense, wait another 24 hours before sampling your efforts. Stored in cool, dry conditions, it will keep for a couple of months or more, longer in the freezer.

Smoked trout

Farmed trout are sold gutted and de-gilled, and most of the fish will have lost the plate of bone behind the gills from which they can be suspended, tail down, in the smoker. Trout fishermen, however, have the option of opening the fish down one side of the spine to clean it kipper-fashion, which makes for more even curing and smoking. This is the ideal treatment for fish weighing up to 500g (1lb) each. Larger trout are better smoked in fillets, like sides of smoked salmon.

CURING **ABOUT 5 HOURS PLUS MAKING AND CHILLING THE BRINE**
SMOKING **12–24 HOURS**

Makes 12
12 very fresh trout, gutted weight 300–450g (10–14½oz) each

FOR THE BRINE
1.35kg (2lb 10oz) sea salt
5 litres (8 pints) water

FOR DRY-SALTING
2kg (4lb) sea salt

1 The brine needs to be well chilled before the fish are added to it, so start the day before. Put the salt and water in a non-reactive container and bring slowly to the boil, stirring to dissolve the salt. Skim, cool and then chill.
2 Wash and dry the fish and put them in the chilled brine for 3 hours for the smaller fish, 4 for larger ones. Wash them under a cold tap and dry with kitchen paper.
3 Strew a layer of salt over the base of a clean container large enough to hold the fish in 1 or 2 layers, and pack in the fish, salting them liberally inside and out. Cover them with salt. Leave in a cool place for just 40 minutes in the case of the smaller fish, 1 hour for larger ones.
4 Wash and dry the fish again. To hang them up, use a trussing needle to thread a loop of string through the flesh near the tail, and tie the string tightly around the tail, making a loop from which to suspend the fish. Pin open the rib cage with toothpicks, or blackthorns gathered when you picked sloes for sloe gin.
5 Fire up the smoker and hang the fish in it making sure that they don't touch each other or the sides. Smoke them for 12–24 hours, ideally in the temperature range 21–26°C (70–79°F) – the smoke takes longer to penetrate in cold, damp weather.
6 Fish smoked like this will keep well in the fridge for 1 week or more.

Tip
Savour cold-smoked trout like smoked salmon, without further cooking, serving with lemon or horseradish cream. But once cold smoked, the freshwater trout resembles sea fish, and is even better treated like finnan haddock and cooked either by poaching in milk and served with a poached egg, or simply wrapped loosely in foil and baked for 15–25 minutes in an oven preheated to 180°C (160°C fan oven/350°F), gas mark 4.

Smoked trout fishcakes with tartare sauce

These fishcakes are also very good when made with hot-smoked salmon.

1 Cook the potatoes in salted boiling water for 15–20 minutes until tender. Drain and leave to steam in the colander for 2 minutes to dry out. Mash the potatoes with the butter and mustard. Leave until cool enough to handle.

2 Carefully stir in the trout and herbs. Divide the mixture into 8 balls, then flatten each ball into a circle about 2cm (¾ inch) deep.

3 Put the seasoned flour, egg, and breadcrumbs into separate bowls. Dust the fishcakes with flour, dip into the egg, then coat with the breadcrumbs. Chill for 30 minutes.

4 Meanwhile, make the tartare sauce. Mix together all of the ingredients and season to taste.

5 Put the oil in a large frying pan to the depth of about 2cm (¾ inch) and set over a low to medium heat. Fry the fishcakes for 5–6 minutes a side until golden and heated through. Serve with the tartare sauce and lemon wedges.

PREPARATION **35 MINUTES PLUS CHILLING**
COOKING **ABOUT 30 MINUTES**

Serves 4

1kg (2lb) floury potatoes, such as King Edward or Maris Piper
50g (2oz) butter
1 teaspoon wholegrain mustard
375g (12oz) Smoked Trout (see opposite), flaked
1 tablespoon each chopped chives and parsley
seasoned flour
2 medium eggs, beaten
100–150g (3½–5oz) fresh breadcrumbs
sunflower or vegetable oil, for frying
lemon wedges, to serve

FOR THE TARTARE SAUCE

150g (5oz) fresh mayonnaise
1 tablespoon capers, rinsed and chopped
6 cornichons, rinsed and chopped
1 shallot, finely chopped
1 tablespoon freshly chopped parsley
a squeeze of lemon juice
salt and freshly ground black pepper

Making sausages

It is easy to make sausages that taste very good indeed, but a little harder to get the texture right, although that, too, is a matter of personal preference. I want fresh sausages to be succulent and juicy, meaty without being too chewy and certainly not tough. Dried, salami-style sausages, which are not cooked but cured and have big, complex flavours, should be chewy without being leathery, and firm enough to cut into wafer-thin slices. Both fresh and dried sausages start with good pork, at least outdoor-reared and preferably organic. Though breed and diet combine to produce unique flavours, the practical choice is to use the best that's available locally, and not too lean. The beauty of homemade sausages is that they contain only good meat, which includes the fat, and no bits you'd rather not eat if you could identify them. Without sufficient fat, sausages are dry and dull, so fat phobics should read no further and turn their talents to making yogurt or bread. Cooks' perks are the bits that get stuck around the auger of the mincer or sausage stuffer. Formed into small, quickly fried patties, they preview the feast to come. And if your taste buds are alert, they also demonstrate the improvement a day's hanging can make to the flavour of a string of homemade sausages.

INGREDIENTS

It is no bad idea to order the meat in advance, particularly if you need hard, pork back fat to dice for dried sausages. The quantities of salt, herbs and spices used in sausages are small so why not use the best – **fine sea salt**, freshly ground **peppercorns** and **fresh herbs**? **Sausage skins** can be natural casings – cleaned intestines preserved in salt – or manufactured casings made from animal collagen. The best casings are natural as they are stronger and more porous than synthetic versions. Hog casings are the size for traditional sausages, and sheep casings for slimmer chipolatas. Larger sizes are needed for dried sausages that will shrink by about a third as they cure. Beef middles are a larger casing, good for homemade salamis where curing temperatures can't be accurately controlled and where the meat needs to be tightly packed to stop harmful bacteria developing in air pockets. The point being that the bigger and, particularly, thicker the sausage, the longer it takes to cure and the greater the risk of failure – going off or growing the wrong moulds before ready.

Specialist ingredients are used in dried sausages to inhibit the growth of harmful organisms during the slow curing process. As the sausages dry, they will develop a white mould on the surface – this is harmless and a good sign that they are maturing properly. **Curing salts**, which replace the saltpetre in old recipes, and **salami starter** are available with instructions by mail order. **Acidophilus powder** can be liberated from capsules sold by pharmacies. For casings, ingredients and equipment (see page 192).

EQUIPMENT

Sausage-making demands high standards of kitchen hygiene and keeping every item of equipment spotlessly clean. Although it is possible to make sausages with just a **knife** to chop the meat and a **funnel** to fill the sausage skins, that really is doing things the hard way and I'd say a **mincer** and **sausage stuffer** are essential. I use the mincing attachment of my trusty electric food mixer that has three sharp metal cutting discs with fine, medium and coarse holes, and plastic sausage-stuffing nozzles in two sizes. Alternatives include a **hand-cranked mincer** plus a **hand-cranked sausage stuffer**, or powered versions of both, which are larger and designed for farm shop or artisan producer use. You'll also need accurate **scales** and **measuring jug**, **sharp knives**, scrubbable **boards**,

adequate fridge space and plenty of hot water. In this case, a clean apron is to protect the food not your frock. To make cured sausages, you will need a **cool, dark, well-ventilated area** so that they can be left to hang and dry for several weeks. Try to maintain a constant temperature between 10°C and 15°C (50°F and 59°F) to prevent uneven drying. To prevent the sausages bulging as they are drying, turn them upside down a few times during the first few weeks.

STUFFING SAUSAGES

• The salted sausage casings need to be soaked in warm water for about 30 minutes before attaching one end to a tap and running cold water through its length to rinse thoroughly.
• Allow a good 2m (6½ft) of hog casing per 1kg (2lb) of sausagemeat.
• Slide the wet casing onto the sausage-stuffing nozzle of a stand mixer or sausage stuffer and place a large clean tray underneath to collect the sausages.
• For the next stage, two pairs of hands are useful. Fill the machine with the prepared sausagemeat and start the motor or crank manually.
• As soon as the sausage mixture begins to come through, tie a knot in the casing and, gently holding it back against the nozzle, let the casing fill plumply.
• To make the links, twist 15–20cm (6–8 inch) lengths in alternate directions as they fill.
• Traditionally, sausages and salamis are made in cold winter weather when flies are scarce. To protect fresh sausages I fashioned a simple hanging larder rather like a fisherman's keepnet from a pair of hula hoops and a length of curtain net. Making salami is still best saved for the cooler months.

A BIT OF TECHNIQUE

• Careful cooking ensures succulent, well-flavoured sausages. Overcooking dries and toughens them. Whether baked, fried or grilled, aim to cook sausages to an internal temperature of 70°C (158°F).
• Lightly cooking onions or garlic in a little butter before adding (chilled) to a sausage mix, makes for a richer, more subtle flavour than adding them raw.

Top left: mincing shoulder of pork.
Top right: adding water to the sausage.
Bottom left: soaking the sausage casings before use.
Bottom right: filling the casings until plump.

Sausages with beans and rosemary

This dish works well with most flavours of fresh sausages; the beans can be varied to suit your taste.

PREPARATION **20 MINUTES**
COOKING **45 MINUTES**

Serves 4
2 tablespoons sunflower oil
8 fresh sausages (see opposite)
1 onion, chopped
1 celery stick, chopped
1 garlic clove, crushed
1 teaspoon tomato purée
1 teaspoon fennel seeds
400g (13oz) tin chopped tomatoes
1 bay leaf
a pinch of sugar
300g (10oz) tin cannellini beans, drained
　　and rinsed
300g (10oz) tin borlotti beans, drained
　　and rinsed
salt and freshly ground black pepper
freshly chopped rosemary leaves, to
　　garnish

1 Heat half the oil in a large sauté pan and brown the sausages over a medium heat. Set aside.
2 Add the remaining oil and gently fry the onion and celery for 10 minutes until softened. Add the garlic, tomato purée and fennel seeds and cook for 1 minute.
3 Pour in the tomatoes, an empty tomato tin full of water and the bay leaf. Add the sugar and season well. Bring to the boil, then turn down to a simmer. Add the sausages and cook for 25 minutes.
4 Add the beans and continue cooking for 5 minutes until heated through. Sprinkle with the rosemary to serve.

Best classic sausages

Make the sausages with fatty shoulder of pork, or with half lean pork shoulder and half fatty belly of pork.

PREPARATION **1½ HOURS PLUS CHILLING AND DRYING**

Makes 1.2kg (2½lb) sausages
1kg (2lb) fatty shoulder of pork without
　　skin or bones
10–15g (¼–½oz) sea salt
1 generous teaspoon freshly ground
　　black or white pepper
1 teaspoon freshly grated nutmeg
100ml (3½fl oz) chilled water
100g (3½oz) fresh white breadcrumbs

1 Cut the meat into large dice or strips that will feed easily through the mincer. Combine with the salt, pepper and nutmeg and mix. Cover and chill for at least 12 hours.
2 Keeping everything as cold as possible, mince the mixture through the fine or medium holes of a mincer.
3 Mix for 1 minute, stirring briskly with a wooden spoon, or use a food mixer with its basic mixing paddle on low speed.
4 Increasing the speed to medium, add the water and mix for 1 minute until the liquid is incorporated. Sprinkle over the breadcrumbs and mix for another minute until they are well blended in and the mixture is firm and rather sticky.
5 Fry a teaspoonful of the sausagemeat (keeping the bulk chilled) to test for seasoning and adjust it if required. Be sure to mix in any additional seasoning very thoroughly.
6 Stuff into prepared hog casings, twisting every 15–20cm (6–8 inches). Cook and eat the sausages freshly made. Alternatively, they will keep, hung in a cool, airy place, for between 12 hours and 2 days, depending on the temperature.

Tip
For a quick one-pan meal, put the Classic Sausages in a roasting pan with 1 tablespoon sunflower oil. Add a couple of red onions, cut into wedges, and a few bay leaves. Season. Bake in the oven at 200°C (180°C fan oven/400°F), gas mark 6 for 25–30 minutes, turning occasionally, until golden and cooked through.

French country sausages

This is an all-meat sausage, robustly flavoured with wine and garlic, and just the job for a cassoulet.

PREPARATION 1½ HOURS PLUS CHILLING AND DRYING

Makes 1.2kg (2½lb) sausages
1kg (2lb) fatty shoulder of pork without skin or bones
10–15g (¼–½oz) sea salt
1 generous teaspoon coarsely ground black pepper
1 tablespoon very finely chopped garlic
100ml (3½fl oz) robust red wine, chilled

1 Cut the meat into large dice or strips that will feed easily through the mincer. Combine the meat with the salt, pepper and garlic and mix thoroughly. Cover and chill for at least half a day and up to 24 hours.

2 Keeping everything as cold as possible, mince the mixture through the fine or medium holes of a mincer into a bowl.

3 Mix for 1 minute, stirring vigorously with a wooden spoon, or using a standing food mixer fitted with its basic mixing paddle on low speed.

4 Increasing the mixer speed to medium, add the wine and mix for another minute until the liquid is incorporated and the mixture is sticky.

5 Fry a teaspoonful of the mixture (keeping the bulk chilled) to test the seasoning and adjust it if required – making sure to mix in any additional seasoning very thoroughly.

6 Stuff into prepared hog casings, twisting every 15–20cm (6–8 inches). Hang the sausages in a cool, airy place for between 12 hours and 2 days, depending on the temperature.

Basic salami

Salami is an inspired way of preserving meat without refrigeration.

PREPARATION 1½ HOURS PLUS CHILLING
DRYING 4 OR MORE WEEKS

Makes 725g (1lb 7oz) salami
800g (1lb 10oz) lean organic pork
  shoulder
200g (7oz) pork back fat, finely diced
1 teaspoon freshly ground black pepper
1 teaspoon fennel seeds, coarsely
  crushed
20g (¾oz) finely ground sea salt
1 garlic clove, crushed to a paste
1 teaspoon acidophilus powder,
  or salami starter (see page 172)
200ml (7fl oz) robust red wine

1 Mince the pork coarsely into a chilled bowl and add the fat. Sprinkle with the pepper and fennel seeds. Mix the salt, garlic and acidophilus powder or salami starter with the wine in a small container and stir until the salt has dissolved. Add the liquid to the meat and mix very thoroughly to distribute it evenly. Chill for several hours or overnight, then mix again before filling the casings.
2 Soak and rinse the casings, ideally beef middles, and slide a length on to the sausage-stuffing nozzle. Knot the end of the casing, then above this, tie on a 50cm (10 inch) piece of string. Fill a 30cm (12 inch) length and, leaving enough unfilled casing to tie another knot, cut it off. Squeeze the wet filling down firmly before knotting the end and securing this by tying another length of string to it.
3 With a sterile pin, prick the filled skins to puncture any air pockets. Note the weight of each sausage.
4 Hang the salamis in a cool place to dry (ideally 15°C/59°F), avoiding extremes of humidity or lack of it, for 4 or more weeks. They are ready when they feel firm right to the centre and have lost about 30% of their weight.

Tip
Once the salami is ready to eat, it can be wrapped in greaseproof paper and refrigerated. Rolling in fine wood ash from a log fire is a traditional added preservative. Vacuum packing also prolongs the life of cured sausages.

Saucisson sec

A coarsely cut and simply seasoned French country sausage that allows the quality of good pork to shine.

PREPARATION 1 HOUR PLUS CHILLING
DRYING 4 OR MORE WEEKS

Makes about 700g (1lb 7oz) saucisson
sec
1kg (2lb) organic boneless shoulder of
  pork, chilled
110g (3½oz) pork back fat, chilled
20g (¾oz) finely ground sea salt
1½ teaspoons coarsely ground black
  pepper
2 teaspoons sugar
½ teaspoon curing salts (organic
  dry-cure for bacon)
1 garlic clove, crushed to a paste

1 Mince the pork and fat coarsely into a chilled bowl. Add the remaining ingredients and mix very thoroughly. Chill for several hours or overnight, then mix very thoroughly again before filling the casings.
2 Fill, finish and mature as for salami.

Terrines and pâtés

A pork pie is a pâté because it is baked in a pastry crust, and brawn is a terrine because it is set in a dish. At least that is the theory. But both words have for so long been interchangeable that the distinction is obsolete and French cooks resort to the belt and braces *pâté en croûte* when a pastry case is called for. If you are now pondering the persistence of the French terms pâté and terrine in plain-speaking kitchens, you may agree that cold meat loaf just doesn't cut it. Why make your own when the deli counter has so many to choose from? For all the usual good reasons – superb flavours, economy and good ingredients with no dodgy bits or dubious additives. Then there's the panache of putting a big dish of pâté on the table with crusty bread, a bowl of salad and a bottle of wine.

Terrine of duck (see pages 182–183)

INGREDIENTS

Pâtés and terrines are traditionally made with cheaper cuts of meat, such as **belly of pork** and **offal,** particularly **liver.** Fat is a virtue in pâté mixtures, especially when liver and lean meats are used, too. It is traditional to line terrines with fat – often thin slices of **streaky bacon** or **pancetta** since it has become so difficult to procure pork caul (the fatty membrane from a pig's stomach) or back fat. However, it is worth talking to your butcher who should be able to order some for you. **Pork fat** is preferable as it has a fairly neutral taste that will mingle well with other flavours and retains a smooth, firm texture and white colour during cooking. An easy alternative is to line the dish with cling film.

Buy only the freshest specimens for a **fish terrine.** The raw flesh tends to be sieved for a fine texture, then combined with **eggs, cream** and **herbs** before being cooked in a bain marie. The result is a delicate mousse just firm enough to slice. **Salmon** is the most popular type of fish-based terrine.

Vegetable terrines are a colourful, fresh alternative but are best served on the day they're made. They're usually created with three different pre-cooked chopped or puréed vegetables, combined with eggs and herbs. Again, they are gently cooked in a bain marie where the egg sets and binds the layers. Blanched whole vegetables such as asparagus, French beans and broccoli florets can also be layered in among the purées.

Small amounts of **wine** and **spirits,** such as **brandy,** add great flavour and, of course, the alcohol cooks off completely. **Spices,** as always, are most fragrant when freshly ground.

EQUIPMENT

A **mincer** is the tool of choice for making most types of pâté. For smooth, creamy mousselines or parfaits – mixtures that would once have been worked through a sieve – a **food processor** is invaluable. However, be careful not to overprocess – the end result should be a purée rather than a paste. It does take time and extra elbow grease but if I'm making a fish terrine I will always **sieve** the mixture rather than use a food processor – it's worth it for the light and airy texture.

A **terrine** takes its name from the earthenware dish it was traditionally cooked in. They are usually a narrow rectangular shape, with deep sides tapering slightly towards the base, and holding between 1kg (2lb) and 1.5kg (3lb). These are ideal for producing pretty slices of layered ingredients. **Loaf tins** without seams can be substituted, as can small casseroles. A probe **thermometer** with a digital read-out takes the guesswork out of cooking temperatures – so there is no longer any need to play safe and risk overcooking the pâté, which results in too much of the fat melting out and leaving the body of the mixture dry and crumbly. Alternatively, test for doneness by inserting a **skewer** into the centre and holding it there for 10 seconds; if the terrine is cooked through the skewer will be hot. A **wooden board** and **heavy scale weights** are used for pressing the terrine after it is cooked– heavy tins make a good substitute.

A BIT OF TECHNIQUE

- Chilling ingredients, mincer and mixer tools, and keeping everything cold until it goes into the oven, helps to improve the texture of the finished pâté.
- Pick over the meat well before mincing or layering as whole strips: gristle, membrane or fibrous strands won't mince properly or won't be pleasant to chew in the finished dish.
- Terrines tend to be cooked in a water bath (bain marie), which is just a large roasting dish deep enough to contain the terrine. Sufficient boiling water is poured around the terrine to come half-way up the sides, then the dish is put into the oven to cook. Cooking the terrine in this way means that the heat is distributed at an even, gentle rate throughout the dish. Top up with extra boiling water if necessary.
- Seasoning needs to be assertive in dishes eaten cold, so always cook a spoonful of the mixture to check. It is best to poach the test piece wrapped up like a toffee in cling film, then allow it to cool before tasting. Return the bulk of the mixture back to the fridge to keep cold.
- Terrines benefit from maturing and chilling in the fridge after cooking for a couple of days to allow the flavours to mingle.

Clarifying butter

Butter has a lower burning point than other fats but clarifying it first enables you to use it to fry food at higher temperatures. To make clarified butter, melt a block of butter in a small pan over a low heat until liquid. It will separate into three layers: white foam, a thick yellow middle layer and a milky white sediment at the bottom. Skim off the white foam and discard. Carefully pour off the yellow clarified butter into a bowl. Discard the sediment.

Terrine of duck

Leave plenty of time for making this terrine before serving: once it's cooked, it needs a couple of days in the fridge to allow the flavours to mingle.

PREPARATION **1½ HOURS PLUS CHILLING**
COOKING **ABOUT 2 HOURS**

Makes about 1.2kg (2½lb)

1 duck, about 2kg (4lb), ideally with giblets
2 tablespoons brandy or Calvados
500g (1lb) belly of pork
250g (8oz) duck or chicken livers, cleaned
50g (2oz) shallot, finely chopped
1 garlic clove, finely chopped
2 teaspoons each sea salt and freshly ground black pepper
6 tablespoons white port or dry white wine
1 bay leaf
a few juniper berries, to decorate

FOR THE STOCK

the duck carcass, skin and giblets, and skin from the pork belly (if available)
1 small leek, chopped
1 carrot, chopped
2 celery sticks, chopped
2 fresh thyme sprigs
a handful parsley
1 bay leaf
150ml (¼ pint) dry white wine
½ teaspoon salt
½ teaspoon black peppercorns

TO FINISH

125ml (4fl oz) well-flavoured duck stock (see above)
2 leaves gelatine (if needed, see method)

1 Cut the legs and wings from the duck, and remove the breast meat, then skin it. Slice the breast meat lengthways into strips about 1cm (½ inch) wide. Put them in a dish with the brandy or Calvados, cover and chill for 1–2 hours or, ideally, overnight.

2 Take the leg and wing meat off the bones and keep it cold.

3 To make the stock, put the carcass, skin, giblets (except the heart and liver) and pork skin in a stock pot and cover with cold water. Bring slowly to the boil, skim, add the vegetables, herbs, wine and the salt and peppercorns, and simmer for 2 hours. Strain, discard the solids, skim off the fat, return to the pan and reduce slowly over a medium heat to about 300ml (½ pint). Cool and then chill it. If the stock included the pork skin, it should set to firm jelly by itself. If not, add the gelatine when melting the stock to seal the terrine (see step 10).

4 Meanwhile, preheat the oven to 150°C (130°C fan oven/300°F), gas mark 2.

5 Using the fine blade of the mincer, mince the meat from the duck legs and wings with the pork, livers and duck heart and liver if you have them. Add the shallot, garlic, salt, pepper and port or wine. Stir vigorously, by hand or machine, until the mixture holds together in a sticky mass.

6 Cook (preferably poach, see page 180) a spoonful of the mixture to test for seasoning. If more is needed, be sure to mix it in very thoroughly.

7 Line a 1.2kg (2½lb) dish with cling film, leaving plenty draped over the edges. Spoon a third of the mixture into the dish and press it well down to eliminate any air pockets. Lay half the marinated duck breast strips lengthways in the terrine and top with another third of the mixture. Repeat with the rest of the strips and finish with pâté mixture, mounding the top in a dome. Lay a bay leaf on top and cover with the cling film. Now add a lid or close covering of foil.

8 Set the terrine in a larger, deep roasting tin and pour in hot tap water, to come halfway up the sides of the dish, and put it in the preheated oven. Bake for about 2 hours or until a probe thermometer inserted into the centre of the pâté reads 75°C (167°F).

9 Take the terrine from the oven and remove from the water bath. Set it in a larger dish and press it under a weight of about 1kg (2lb) until it is cold. Refrigerate for 2–3 days to allow the maximum flavour to develop.

10 The day before serving the terrine, heat the jellied stock to boiling point, simmer it for 5 minutes and leave it to cool down until warm. In the meantime, turn the pâté out of its baking dish, peel off the cling film and dry the pâté by patting it with kitchen paper. Wash and dry the dish, then return the pâté to it. Soak the gelatine leaves (if using) in cold water and stir them into the warm stock. Let the stock cool, but before it starts to set, pour it into the terrine. Decorate with a few juniper berries. Chill.

Tip
The terrine of duck cuts into attractive slices and, for that reason, is finished with jelly (aspic) rather than fat.

Creamy chicken liver pâté

This is a rich, smoothly spreadable pâté to be made, ideally, with fresh organic chicken livers. Present it in a single dish, or in individual servings, with light, crunchy toasts. Sealing the surface with a slick of clarified butter (see page 181) or with jellied stock helps to preserve the pâté's pink tinge and stops it greying.

PREPARATION **30 MINUTES PLUS CHILLING**
COOKING **10 MINUTES**

Serves 6

- 150g (5oz) unsalted butter
- 350g (11½oz) fresh chicken livers, cleaned
- 1 teaspoon freshly chopped tarragon leaves
- 50g (2oz) shallot, finely chopped
- 1 garlic clove, finely chopped
- 2 tablespoons sweet sherry
- 2 tablespoons mascarpone
- salt and freshly ground black pepper

TO FINISH

- 3–4 tablespoons clarified butter or jellied stock (see page 182)
- toast, to serve

1 Heat a sauté pan and add a walnut-sized piece of butter. Add the chicken livers and tarragon and fry quickly, turning them, until they are coloured on the outside but still pink in the centre. Transfer to a blender or food processor.
2 Melt another knob of butter and add the shallot and garlic. Fry them for 2–3 minutes until they are tender and translucent. Pour in the sherry and reduce until only a teaspoon remains. Add this mixture to the processor.
3 Add the mascarpone to the livers and season generously. Process until the

mixture is smooth, then leave it to cool until the bowl is no longer warm to the touch. With the processor running, add the remaining butter, in 2–3 batches, and continue processing until the pâté is very smooth. Add seasoning to taste and divide the mixture between 6 small dishes. Cover and chill.
4 As soon as the pâté is cold, run a thin layer of clarified butter or jellied stock over the surface. Chill, then bring to room temperature and serve with toast.

Rustic pork terrine

A slice of this terrine served with a few homegrown salad leaves and crunchy cornichons makes a simple, but deeply satisfying light lunch.

PREPARATION **1 HOUR**
COOKING **ABOUT 2 HOURS**

Makes about 1.5kg (3lb)

1kg (2lb) belly of pork
500g (1lb) pig's liver
2 garlic cloves, finely chopped
100g (3½oz) shallot, finely chopped
½ teaspoon ground mace
1 tablespoon sea salt
1 tablespoon whole green peppercorns, rinsed
100ml (3½fl oz) dry white wine
2 tablespoons brandy
150g (5oz) thinly sliced rashers pancetta or green streaky bacon
1 bay leaf

1 Preheat the oven to 150°C (130°C fan oven/300°F), gas mark 2.
2 Mince the pork and liver using the coarse or medium blade of a mincer and add the garlic, shallot, mace, salt, green peppercorns, wine and brandy. Stir vigorously by hand or machine until the mixture starts to hold together in a sticky mass.
3 Cook (see page 180) a spoonful of the mixture to test for seasoning. If more is needed, mix it in thoroughly.
4 Line a 1.5kg (3lb) terrine with bacon, leaving plenty draped over the edges to fold over the top. Spoon the mixture into the dish, pressing down well and finishing with a mounded top. Top with a bay leaf and fold the bacon over. Now add a lid or close covering of foil.
5 Set the terrine in a roasting tin, pour in hot tap water to come halfway up the sides of the dish and bake for about 2 hours, or until a probe thermometer inserted into the centre of the pâté reads 75°C (167°F).
6 Remove from the oven and the water bath. Set the terrine in a larger dish and press it under a weight of about 1kg (2lb) until it is cold. Refrigerate for 2–3 days for maximum flavour to develop.

Mushroom pâté

A few dried wild mushrooms add greatly to the flavour of this spreadable pâté made with a mixture of cultivated mushrooms. Though a large panful of fungi makes a relatively small quantity of pâté, what it lacks in bulk it delivers fully in taste.

PREPARATION **15 MINUTES PLUS SOAKING**
COOKING **15 MINUTES**

Serves 6
10g (¼oz) dried ceps or other wild
**   mushrooms**
30g (1¼oz) unsalted butter
50g (2oz) shallot, finely chopped
400g (13oz) fresh mixed mushrooms,
**   sliced**
½ teaspoon salt
1 teaspoon fresh thyme leaves
2 tablespoons mascarpone
a dash of Tabasco sauce
2 teaspoons fresh lemon juice
2 teaspoons truffle oil (optional)

1 Soak the dried mushrooms in 100ml (3½fl oz) boiling water for 30 minutes or more.
2 In a large sauté pan over a lowish heat, melt the butter and sauté the shallot until it is soft. Raise the heat and add the sliced mushrooms, keeping them moving until they begin to fry and give off some moisture. Add the soaked mushrooms, their liquor, salt and the thyme. Cook, stirring, over a high heat until the mixture is completely dry.
3 Leave to cool completely before processing with the mascarpone, Tabasco and a teaspoon each of lemon juice and truffle oil. Taste before adding more, if you like. Transfer to a sterilized kilner jar for storing.

Tip
Spread small crackers with a dab of mascarpone, a spoonful of mushroom pâté and a sliver of Parmesan.

Potted prawns or shrimps

Use tiny sweet brown shrimps if you can get hold of them or small North Atlantic prawns.

PREPARATION **10 MINUTES PLUS CHILLING**
COOKING **2–3 MINUTES**

Serves 2–3
150g (5oz) unsalted butter
225g (7½oz) cooked small prawns or
**   shrimps**
a pinch of cayenne pepper
a squeeze of lemon juice
salt and freshly ground black pepper

1 Heat the butter over a medium heat until melted and it stops sizzling – don't let it go brown. Skim away the froth. Pour the clear, golden (clarified) butter into a bowl, leaving behind the milky solids in the bottom of the pan.
2 Toss the prawns in 1 tablespoon of the clarified butter and mix in the cayenne pepper and lemon juice. Check the seasoning.
3 Pack the prawns into 2–3 ramekins and pour over the remaining butter. Chill until set. Serve with toast. They will keep in the fridge for up to 5 days.

Potted crabmeat

Spread on hot toast for a very pleasing supper or snack.

PREPARATION **15 MINUTES PLUS CHILLING**

Serves 2–3
225g (7½oz) freshly picked white and
**   brown crabmeat**
110g (3½oz) unsalted butter, softened
a pinch of cayenne pepper
1 teaspoon very finely chopped curly
**   parsley**
salt
a squeeze of lemon juice
clarified butter (see page 181)

1 Blend together the crabmeat, butter, cayenne pepper and parsley. Season with salt and fresh lemon juice.
2 Divide between 2–3 small ramekins and cover with a thin layer of clarified butter. Chill and use within 3 days.

INDEX

USEFUL ADDRESSES

General kitchen equipment

NISBETS PLC
Fourth Way,
Avonmouth, Bristol,
BS11 8TB
0845 140 5555
www.nisbets.co.uk

LAKELAND LTD
Alexandra Buildings,
Windermere,
Cumbria LA23 1BQ
015394 88100
www.lakeland.co.uk

**Breadmaking ingredients
and equipment**

For organic flour from 1kg
(2lb) bags to 25kg (50lb)
sacks; proving baskets;
yeast:
DOVES FARM FOODS LTD
Salisbury Road,
Hungerford,
Berkshire RG17 0RF
01488 684880
www.dovesfarm.co.uk

SHIPTON MILL LTD
Long Newnton,
Tetbury,
Gloucestershire GL8 8RP
01666 505050
www.shipton-mill.com

For artisan bakery
equipment: from proving
baskets, baking stones and
tins to peels, paddles and
wood-fried ovens:
BAKERY BITS LTD
1 Orchard Units,
Duchy Road,
Honiton,
Devon EX14 1YD
(By appointment only)
01404 565656
www.bakerybits.co.uk

Preserving equipment

JAM JAR SHOP
25 Pillings Road,
Oakham,
Rutland,
LE15 6QF 01572 720720
www.jamjarshop.com

WARES OF KNUTSFORD LTD
PO Box 321, Knutsford WA16
8YQ 08456 121273 www.
waresofknutsford.co.uk

Sausage making and casings

www.sausage-casings.co.uk
01942 498200

**A.W.SMITH & SONS
(SUNDRIES) LTD**
The Food Trades Centre,
Unit 21, Stirchley Trading
Estate,
Hazelwell Road,
Stirchley, Birmingham
B30 2PF
0044 0121 486 4500
www.awsmith.co.uk

Antique kitchenalia

**BELOW STAIRS OF
HUNGERFORD**
103 High Street, Hungerford,
Berkshire, RG17 0NB
01488 682317
www.belowstairs.co.uk

JANE WICKS
Country Ways,
Rye, East Sussex
01424 71363

**QUILL FARM AND COUNTRY
ANTIQUES**
Westfield Farm,
Foulsham,
Norfolk NR20 5RH
01362 680147

Smoking equipment

OUTDOOR COOK
37 High Street,
Lewes,
East Sussex BN7 2LU.
01273 782447
www.outdoorcook.co.uk

FOR FOOD SMOKERS
28 New Road,
Gomshall,
Surrey GU5 9LZ
01483 203095
www.forfoodsmokers.co.uk

ACKNOWLEDGEMENTS

I would like to thank the following people for their help
with this book:

Tara Fisher for her wonderful photographs and Caroline
Reeves for her stunning and creative propping – a team who
were a true pleasure to work with and who made my task
of food styling so much easier. The team at Jacqui Small:
Kerenza Swift, Abi Waters and Ashley Western for pulling the
whole book together so beautifully and being so patient with
me. The team at Country Living magazine – just for being
great. Most of all, my husband, Keith, and my Mum and Dad
for believing in me when I decided to retrain at Leiths School
of Food & Wine to realize my dream of becoming a food
writer. This book is for you. Thank you.

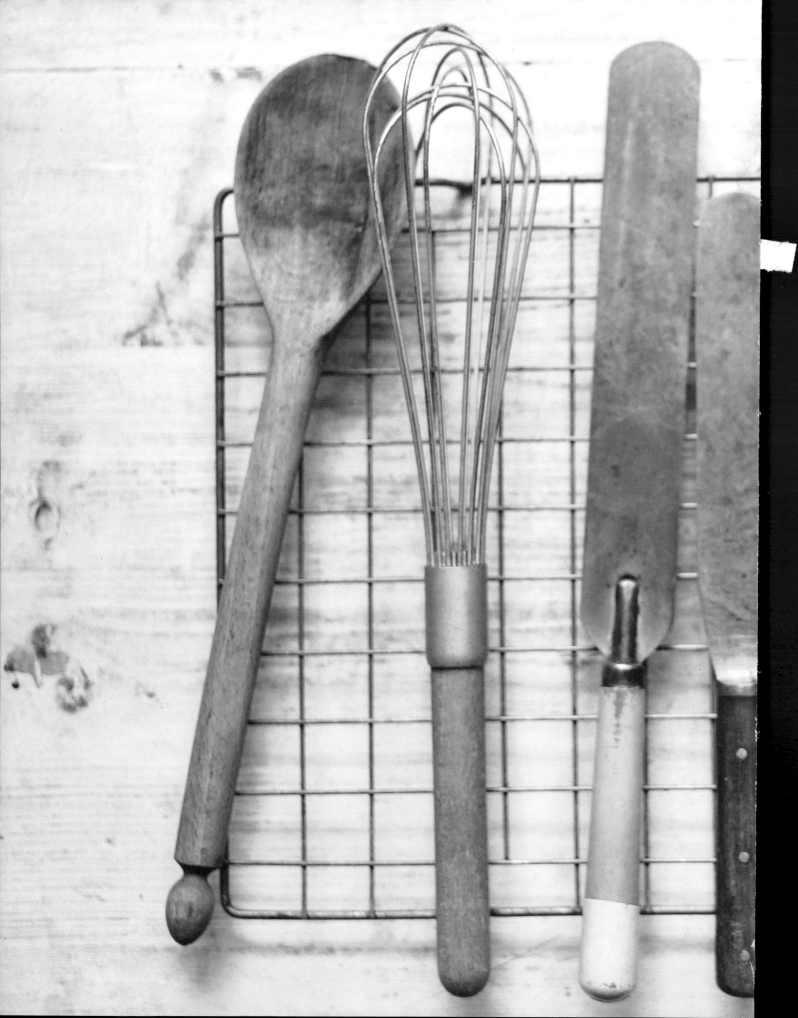